THE

WELSH PEAKS

A Pictorial Guide to walking in
this region and to the safe ascent
of its principal mountain groups

by

W. A. POUCHER, F.R.P.S.

with

235 photographs by the author

14 Maps and 52 Routes

Fifth Edition

LONDON
CONSTABLE & CO. LTD.

D1391393

427341 041 (6)

First published 1962
Second Edition 1965
Third Edition 1967
Fourth Edition 1970
Fifth Edition 1973

© 1962 by William Arthur Poucher

ISBN 0 09 459300 0

The author is a member of
The Climbers' Club
The Fell & Rock Climbing Club

MADE AND PRINTED IN GREAT BRITAIN BY
EBENEZER BAYLIS & SON LTD.
LEICESTER AND LONDON

THE WELSH PEAKS

Plate 1. ROUTE 18—TRYFAN IN WINTER RAIMENT

PREFACE TO THE FIFTH EDITION

IN the second edition of this work I drew attention to the problem of access to the Y Garn end of the Nantlle Ridge, as there was then no Right of Way despite its undisputed use for over half a century. I had hoped that the purchase by the Welsh Office of the ex-Vaynol Estate lands would have facilitated access negotiations, but at the time of writing they had made no progress. Hence, all wayfarers should ignore Route 43 for the time being, and give the ridge a wide berth so as not to exacerbate this delicate situation.

Access to Mynydd Mawr has now been temporarily agreed and Route 44 has been amended to conform to the modified line of approach.

In previous editions, up to and including the 3rd, Route 24 started at Nant Peris and reached Glyder Fawr by way of Llyn y Cwn, but owing to difficulties of access it was removed from the 4th edition and replaced by the ascent of Elidar Fawr. As the present edition goes to press I learn that the footpath from Gwastadnant, Nant Peris, has recently been reopened and waymarked through the enclosed land from the bi-lingual sign in the Llanberis Pass, but it now goes to the R of the stream and waterfall shown previously. In these changed circumstances I shall hope to reintroduce this Route in the next edition.

I would like to draw attention to the valuable work done to improve the amenities of the Park by the National Park warden service which includes both full-time and voluntary wardens. The Warden Service has taken part and supervised a number of voluntary work parties in making good footpaths, including digging out storm water culverts and waymarking, etc.

It appears that on completion thoughtless walkers sometimes amuse themselves by filling up the ditches and blocking the culverts which result in even more flooding. Will any reader who happens to observe such needless mischief please endeavour to stop it and so contribute to the conservation of this esteemed mountain region.

In view of the vast scope of this book it is obviously impossible to check frequently every one of the descriptions of the routes. Time, usage, rock falls and local weather may be responsible for slight variations and should any reader encounter any inaccuracy I would appreciate a note of it for inclusion in future editions of this work.

It should be noted that the Routes described and illustrated herein have been frequented over the years without objection, but they do not necessarily constitute a Right of Way. If in doubt, the reader should contact the owner of the land and ask permission to cross it before embarking upon his walk. This is most important in view of the scourge of vandalism now sweeping the country, which has resulted in damage to fences, hedges, gates, walls, cairns and shelters in mountainous districts; which is not only deplorable but also contrary to the accepted Country Code.

Finally, I would urge Leaders of school and youth parties not to venture on these hills unless the weather is favourable, and moreover, they should always insist upon everyone wearing boots and proper clothing. For, by doing so they will not only reduce the risk of accidents but also avoid the often needless call for Mountain Rescue.

A suggestion for a ROUTE CARD appears at the end of this volume and its use by every walker and climber could help to reduce the number of casualties on our peaks. Please report your route to your lodgings and do not deviate from it.

W. A. POUCHER

4 Heathfield,
Reigate Heath, Surrey

The maps in this Guide are reproduced from the Ordnance Survey Maps with the sanction of the Controller of Her Majesty's Stationery Office. Crown copyright reserved.

CONTENTS

	Page
FRONTISPIECE. Tryfan in winter raiment	2
PREFACE	5
INTRODUCTORY NOTES	9
EQUIPMENT	11
Boots, Clothes, Rucksacks, Maps, Compass, Aneroid, Ice Axe	
ROCK CLIMBING	19
Club Huts	
THE WELSH CENTRES	
Snowdonia. Betws-y-coed, Capel Curig, Ogwen Cottage, Bethesda, Pen-y-gwryd, Pen-y-pass, Llanberis, Beddgelert, The Snowdon Ranger	21
Mid-Wales. Dolgellau, Tal-y-llyn, Dinas Mawddwy, Bala, Harlech, Llanbedr, Barmouth, The Devil's Bridge	24
South Wales. Abergavenny, Crickhowell, Talgarth, Hay, Brecon, Storey Arms	26
GLOSSARY OF WELSH PLACE-NAMES	27
THE WELSH PEAKS	33
Group System for 52 Routes of Ascent	
HEIGHTS OF THE PEAKS	36
72 Tops arranged according to Altitude	
THE PRINCIPAL WELSH LAKES	38
MOUNTAIN PHOTOGRAPHY	41
13 Essentials for good Mountain Pictures	

	page
PHOTOGRAPHY IN THE DIFFERENT GROUPS	52
The best Pictorial Views *of* the groups	
The most Striking Views *from* the groups	
NOTES ON THE ROUTES	58
The 12 Mountain Groups, The Routes, Descents, The Panoramas	
DISTANCES AND TIMES	59
Formula for calculating Distances and Times with an example of the Snowdon Horseshoe which includes Routes 1 and 4	
ROUTE FINDING IN MIST	61
ACCIDENT PROCEDURE	62
BROCKEN SPECTRES	63
GLORIES	63
DETAILED DIRECTIONS FOR 52 ROUTES	
The Snowdon Group. 10 Routes and 56 Photographs	63
The Glyders Group. 16 Routes and 47 Photographs	135
The Carneddau. 9 Routes and 40 Photographs	200
The Moel Siabod Group. 6 Routes and 24 Photographs	253
The Moel Hebog Group. 3 Routes and 26 Photographs	287
Cadair Idris. 1 Route and 7 Photographs	323
The Harlech Dome. 2 Routes and 7 Photographs	337
The Arennigs. 1 Route and 3 Photographs	351
The Arans. 1 Route and 5 Photographs	358
Plynlimon. 1 Route and 2 variations and 4 Photographs	369
The Black Mountains. 1 Route and 4 Photographs	378
The Brecon Beacons. 1 Route and 5 Photographs	387
INDEX	397
ROUTE CARD	403

INTRODUCTORY NOTES

THE coastal resorts of Wales have been a treasured venue for the holidaymaker for many decades, and with the increased interest in mountain walking and rock climbing Snowdonia too has achieved an immense popularity that is second to none in this country. But the remote and wild landscape of South and Mid-Wales has for some inexplicable reason escaped this attention, despite the magnificence of the scenery, the opportunities for hill walking in comparative solitude, and the possibility of ascents of varying difficulty on its innumerable crags and cliffs. Today accessibility is no excuse for this neglect, because almost all the narrow winding roads leading into the hills have been either improved or resurfaced, and as cars are nowadays within the reach of almost everyone I hope the information given in these pages will lead to a more extensive exploration of the whole of the Principality.

At the present time most of our young people have ample funds available for holidays, and since youth hostelling and camping are an inexpensive form of travel there is no valid reason why this country as a whole should not become as cherished a centre as any other in Britain. Energetic young men and women who have a special predilection for hill country may well choose Snowdonia for their first visit, and on arrival they will raise their eyes to the peaks and imagine themselves standing by one of the summit cairns, inhaling the invigorating mountain air and scanning the valleys far below, the chain of engirdling hills and the distant glimmering seas. Come what may, they lose no time in setting out to climb one of them, and on reaching their objective gain that satisfaction that comes only after the ardours of the ascent. It is highly probable that Snowdon will be their first conquest, not only because it is the monarch of Wales and the countryside as far north as the border, but also because they believe it will disclose the finest and most comprehensive panorama on account of its dominating altitude. On achieving this ambition, they quite naturally speculate upon the merits of the views from the other high peaks in the region, and after talking over the question with friends they will in all probability continue their exploration by climbing Tryfan, or walking over the Glyders, or perhaps even traversing the fine Nantlle Ridge, on their first vacation.

On returning home they will often ponder over these experiences, and especially so if they have been captivated by the spirit and mystery of the hills. The map will doubt-less be unfolded at frequent intervals, and by tracing the routes thereon they will re-live these happy times. If they climbed Snowdon by the Pyg Track, their thoughts will follow that pleasant route from Pen-y-pass with Crib Goch rising into the sky ahead, their surprise at the fine view of Lliwedd on attaining Bwlch y Moch, the tramp along the stony undulating path with Yr Wyddfa in front and the sudden appearance of Glaslyn below, the scramble up the steep zig-zags to the col where the Snowdon Railway first comes into view, the walk along the edge of the cwm with Snowdon ahead and the exhilaration of finally stand-ing on the large cairn on the roof of Wales with a whole kingdom spread out far below.

A close inspection of the map will suggest to our friends several other routes to this lofty peak, and curiosity will induce them to speculate upon their respective merits. Would the Miners' Track have been more interesting? Perhaps it would have been more thrilling to have made the ascent from the beautiful Vale of Gwynant by the Watkin

Path, or what of the more distant approaches from the Snowdon Ranger Youth Hostel or Rhyd-ddu? Then another line of thought may develop; for they had seen a grand array of peaks engirdling the horizon from Yr Wyddfa and they will speculate again upon the merits of the panoramas from their summits, to realise with surprise that a lifetime is not too long in which to become acquainted with them all.

The cogitations of our young friends will follow a normal course and they will do exactly the same as the rest of us did in our novitiate; for they will formulate the plans for their next holiday long before it is due. Next time they may decide to stay perhaps in Mid-Wales and explore the adjacent hills; but which ones? To solve this problem they will often get out the map, and while scanning it with happy anticipation compare it with the various guide-books which describe this lovely countryside. There they will *read* what their authors have so lucidly written, but much will inevitably be left to their imagination.

It is here that my long experience of the Welsh Peaks will help them to solve their problems, for by consulting this volume in conjunction with my other works devoted to this region they will not only be able to choose their centre with certainty, their routes to the peaks in the vicinity in accordance with their powers as climbers, and their subjects for their cameras if they happen to be photographers, but they will also be able to *see* beforehand through the medium of my camera studies precisely the type of country that will satisfy every one of their needs.

EQUIPMENT

ANYONE who ventures on the hills without proper equipment is asking for trouble, and since the weather is one of our greatest hazards it is wise, and indeed imperative, to

Plate 2

Plate 3

be prepared for sudden changes, as for instance from warm sunshine to rain or blizzard, by wearing proper boots and clothing, as well as other relatively inexpensive but useful incidentals which I shall enumerate in these pages.

Boots are of course the most important item, and every time I ascend Snowdon or Tryfan by one or other of the routes I shall describe later, I am astonished to observe the strange footgear worn by some of our young friends; among which thin leather or rubber-soled shoes are common.

Good climbing boots are expensive, but those who can afford the best will be amply repaid by their comfort and service through years of tough wear. There are several patterns, and since I have already described and illustrated the best type of *Nailed* boots in my *Lakeland Peaks*, I will not repeat the advice here because in recent years tastes have changed and I will therefore now deal only with Vibrams and similar types. Some years ago, on one of my frequent visits to Zermatt, I had a pair of these boots specially made for me by the world-famous Alexander Burgener, who at that time had invented a new system of lacing as shown in the accompanying illustration. Aside from the rubber soles, the main feature was the elimination of any side stitching which might cause undue friction to the ankles, by making the uppers with two pieces of soft leather stitched together at toe and heel. The leather was double, interspersed with soft padding, to reduce shock from contact with rock on either side of the foot. Moreover, he changed the shape of the toe so that during a descent the pressure was evenly distributed over all five toes, and the lacing began at the toes and was secured by hooks on either side so that tightness or looseness could be adjusted to personal requirements. This pattern has since been universally adopted, but improved by using only one piece of leather, stitched at the heel. The use of silicone as a water repellent in boot creams ensures proofing of the leather and thus eliminates treatment with castor oil.

14

There is a choice of rubber sole between Vibrams and Itshide Commandos, and the selection is a matter of taste. In addition, as further security for rock climbing, there are types having No. 6 Tricouni round soles and heels, and even heel plates if preferred. There are advantages and disadvantages in rubber soles without these trimmings: they are silent and easier on the feet on DRY rock, but on WET rock or moss-covered slabs they can be a handicap to rapid progress because the utmost care becomes imperative to avoid a slip which in an exposed situation might result in a twisted or broken ankle. Strong laces are vital and there is a wide choice between nylon, waxed fabric, leather and porpoise; my preference is for the latter because they stand up to all weathers admirably. Stockings and socks are worthy of some attention and one of each worn together ensure comfort and warmth and reduce undue friction. The *colour* of these items may be important and for some years I have worn RED because in case of accident this colour can be seen at a great distance, and in consequence would facilitate location and subsequent rescue. Some readers may smile or even smirk at this suggestion, but it is a factor that if universally adopted could reduce the unhappy toll of our hills.

Clothes are perhaps a matter of personal taste, and there are still many climbers who delight in wearing their oldest cast-off suits, often intentionally with brilliant patches as a decoration! But there is more protection when wearing a properly made *Alpine Jacket*, of which there are a variety of patterns and colours. They are usually made from closely woven cotton of double texture at the main points of friction. They are windproof and reasonably waterproof and perfectly so if treated with silicone or polyurethane. Good models have four pockets, of which two are large enough to accommodate maps which are then kept dry. It is useful to have small pockets under the armpits; one for a compass and the other for camera accessories, both of

15

which cannot get wet in this position. A skirt is now made to all types, and in heavy rain keeps moisture from percolating on to the small of the back. The collar could be lined with wool to keep the neck warm in the absence of a scarf. In the better jackets there is a small zip opening below the back of the neck to accommodate the hood when not in use. Outside belts are no longer worn because they may put a rock climber off-balance by inadvertently catching on a tiny excrescence of crag. They are now universally replaced by a draw cord which runs in a groove at the waist between the double-texture cloth. This type of Alpine Jacket has a zip fastener down the front and goes well up into the neck, whereas *Anoraks* are made in one piece, with a large kangaroo pocket at breast height and a short zip only at the neck. Nylon is now replacing cotton in some models; I have one of double texture, interspersed with nylon wool, and it is exceptionally light and warm. In very stormy weather a *Cagoule* gives the best protection, but despite the vents copious condensation occurs inside. In view of the rapid changes of temperature encountered in hill country, it is always advisable to carry spare *Pullovers*. Those made of light Shetland wool are much better than a heavy one, because the layers of warm air between them maintain the body temperature, and the number worn can be easily adjusted to varying conditions. *String Vests* worn next to the skin have reduced the risks of colds, and by their use the number of pullovers can be cut down considerably. *Leg Gear* is a matter of choice; some climbers swear by trousers while others prefer plus twos. Personally I consider the latter more comfortable and in addition they allow more freedom about the feet. The *material* from which they are made is another consideration. Many have a preference for corduroy, but I do not care for it because it is made of cotton and therefore cold to the skin, and when it gets very wet the material acts like a sponge and retains an excess of moisture. The weight about the legs then increases and is attended by much discomfort. Alternatively, hard wearing and close-woven tweed is warm and light in weight and altogether more amenable in all mountain weather. *Headgear* has changed considerably in recent years, and the feathered, velour Austrian hat is seldom seen nowadays. The more practical and useful protection is at present confined to two types: the woollen brightly coloured *Bob-Cap* and the old-fashioned *Balaclava Helmet*. In fair weather the former functions admirably and will not blow off in a strong wind, whereas the latter is indispensable in Alpine conditions.

Rucksacks are a necessity and may be obtained in a variety of shapes, colours, sizes and weights. If the climber is moving from place to place and wishes to carry spare clothing, incidentals and photographic gadgets, then it must be a large one such as a Bergan, otherwise a small light model should give satisfactory service. Some prefer those having a light metal frame which keeps the sack off the back and so allows plenty of ventilation. In addition I have one with a leather base to both sack and pockets which increases its durability and prolongs its life.

Maps of this extensive region should be the guide and friend of all who climb the Welsh Peaks. There are two series of outstanding merit, and if dissected and mounted on linen they are more easily handled out of doors, but the present cost is so prohibitive that their general use is declining. The one-inch series issued by the Ordnance Survey have the contours at intervals of fifty feet, and at the time of writing the relevant sheets were as follows: No. 107, Snowdonia; No. 116, Cadair Idris, The Arans, The Arennigs and the Harlech Dome; No. 127, Plynlimon; and No. 141, the Black Mountains and the Brecon Beacons. The half-inch series issued by Bartholomew have the contours at intervals of 250 feet, but the splendid layer system of colouring reveals the topography of the country with great clarity. The O.S. maps in this work are marked with the various routes to the peaks and should be of immense value to all climbers.

A Compass should always be carried in the hills, despite the fact that it may not be needed in clear weather if the ground is familiar. In mist, however, all mountains become wrapped in deeper mystery with the complete disappearance of well-known landmarks, and if the climber is off the beaten track he may well find himself in difficulties without one. A good compass is not cheap, but it is money well spent. Mountain photographers should note that certain types of Exposure Meter containing a magnet may deflect the compass needle if the two are within a short distance of one another. Tests I have made indicate that at a distance of 9 inches N, 12 inches E, and 18 inches S and W the magnetic north is deflected, and when the exposure meter is close to the compass the needle simply spins round. Climbers should therefore test the two instruments and keep one well away from the other when in use, as in misty weather incorrect route finding might result and so lead to unforeseen difficulties.

An Aneroid is a most useful instrument and may be a luxury to all save the explorer. A good one is a fairly reliable forecaster of the weather, and since it approximately indicates the altitude it may be a valuable aid in misty weather by helping to locate one's position with greater accuracy. The lower-priced instruments register up to a height of 10,000 feet. If you possess one, always remember to adjust the dial to the altitude of the starting point of your climb, if it is known with certainty, and thereafter check it at any known station. Bear in mind that when the barometer is falling the readings will be too high, and if it is rising they will be too low. In any event the error is about 100 feet for each 1/10 of an inch of rise or fall not due to change of altitude.

An Ice Axe is valuable and may be indispensable in snow

climbing; moreover, it is a useful tool for glissading and its correct employment will ensure a safe and rapid descent of steep snow slopes. There are numerous makes, each of which has some slight variation in design of both pick and adze. A competent dealer will advise on the most suitable type, which is largely governed by length of shaft, weight and balance. A sling is a useful adjunct and may prevent the loss of the axe if it should slip out of the hand when in use.

In conclusion, I would advise everyone venturing on the hills at any time of year to carry the following items which could spell survival in extremely bad weather. (1) Map and compass; (2) torch and whistle; (3) spare food and clothing, including a large polythene bag; and (4) a small first aid kit.

ROCK CLIMBING

North Wales is resplendent with precipitous cliffs of sound rock that in recent years have become the treasured playground of the rock climber. Those of Clogwyn Du'r Arddu, Lliwedd, Craig yr Ysfa, Silyn, Llanberis Pass, Glyder Fach and Idwal afford courses of varying difficulty, and during the holiday season are much favoured by intrepid cragsmen. Courses in South and Mid-Wales are comparatively rare, but a few years ago climbers explored the buttresses and gullies of Craig Cywarch, in the Arans, and doubtless others will follow as interest increases in this sport.

There are thus ample opportunities for the enjoyment of this exhilarating pastime among the Welsh Peaks, but a novice should never attempt it without proper guidance and training. If you have a friend who is an experienced rock climber, ask him to explain its technique and the management of the rope, and at the first opportunity get him to lead you up some of the easy courses, when you will have the chance to put these theories into practice. If you have a steady head, good balance and can acquire

19

the rhythm required for proficiency, he will soon notice it and lead you up routes of greater difficulty until finally you tackle the severes.

Should you become keen on this fascinating sport, you may wish to apply for membership of one of the clubs or associations whose activities are concentrated mainly in Wales. The following information may be helpful, but it should be borne in mind that some of the clubs are already full and unable to consider further applications for membership.

The Climbers' Club was formed in Snowdonia and its objects are to encourage mountaineering and hill walking, to further the interests of science and art in relation thereto, and to guard and promote the general interests of mountaineers. All gentlemen interested in the objects of the club, as defined above, are eligible as members. Candidates for admission must be proposed and seconded by members of not less than two years' standing, who must have personal knowledge of the candidate. There are three club huts in North Wales. Helyg is situated on the Holyhead Road, two and a half miles from Capel Curig; it is near Tryfan and gives easy access to its three fine buttresses. The R. W. Lloyd Hut, Ynys Etws, is situated in the Llanberis Pass, about one and a half miles above the bus terminus at Nant Peris. Cwm Glas Mawr is also in the Llanberis Pass near Blaen-y-nant Farm and about one mile up the valley from the same bus stop. *The Midland Association of Mountaineers* has its headquarters in Birmingham and owns Glandena, a conspicuous hut situated just above the headwaters of Llyn Ogwen and beside the Holyhead Road. *The Rucksack Club* is very active in Manchester and owns Beudy-mawr which is situated in the Llanberis Pass, two and a half miles below Pen-y-pass. Finally there is the *Central Council of Physical Recreation* whose headquarters in Snowdonia are situated at Plas-y-Brenin, just beside the twin Capel Lakes. The main purpose of the centre is to

20

provide residential training in outdoor activities such as rock climbing, mountain walking, map and compass reading, mobile camping, etc. Other clubs, not primarily concerned with Wales, are the *Ramblers' Association* and the *Camping Club,* many of whose members are experienced mountaineers.

THE WELSH CENTRES

IN the following list I have given the principal centres from which the Welsh Peaks may be most conveniently climbed. But it should be borne in mind that strong walkers are often able to reach them from more distant places, and remote Youth Hostels which are occasionally less conveniently situated. At the time of writing there were forty-five hostels in Wales, but I have only cited those giving reasonably easy access to the major hill ranges. Since this region is so vast, I have enumerated the centres under three well-defined mountain areas: Snowdonia, Mid-Wales and South Wales.

SNOWDONIA

Betws-y-coed is the Gateway to Snowdonia for perhaps the majority of visitors, and is well situated on the River Conway at an important road junction. It has also the advantage of a railway connection with Llandudno Junction on the main line from London and the Midlands. Most of the region can be explored by motorists from its many hotels, as one highway leads into the heart of the peaks and the other penetrates the sylvan stretches of the Lledr Valley. It is too far away to be a really convenient centre for the climber, but there is a Youth Hostel at Pont-y-pant on the way to Dolwyddelan.

Capel Curig is exceptionally well placed at the road junction to Llanberis and Bethesda and is an excellent centre for the climber. There are some comfortable hotels, several guest houses and a Youth Hostel. All the peaks are readily accessible to the motorist and buses serve many of them too. Moel Siabod rises almost overhead and the eastern tops of the Carneddau and Glyders are only a short step away.

Ogwen Cottage is situated at the foot of Llyn Ogwen and on the crest of Nant Ffrancon. It stands in the very shadow of the peaks and affords easy access to the Carneddau, the Milestone Buttress, Tryfan, Idwal and the whole of the Glyders. But it is now a Mountain School, owned by the City of Birmingham, and has recently been much enlarged. Climbers desiring further information should write direct to the warden. There is a Youth Hostel nearby.

Bethesda is situated at the foot of Nant Ffrancon and has an hotel and several guest houses. It is too far away from the main peaks for the average pedestrian, but those who wish to be near the western Glyders and the south-western Carneddau will find it a good centre.

Pen-y-gwryd is perhaps the most famous climbers' centre in the whole of Snowdonia, and stands at the junction of the roads to Llanberis and Beddgelert. It is encircled by the lower slopes of Snowdon, the Glyders and Moel Siabod, and thus gives easy access to many of their peaks. The hotel has a long mountaineering history and will always be closely associated with the Climbers' and Pinnacle clubs.

Pen-y-pass is equally well known and is superbly situated on the lofty crest of the Llanberis Pass. It is the starting point for the Snowdon Horseshoe, for other favoured routes to Yr Wyddfa, for the direct ascent of Glyder Fawr and Esgair Felen, and gives easy access to Llyn Llydaw. The name of the distinguished mountaineer Geoffrey Winthrop Young will always be associated with it and also with his famous Easter parties. It is now a

22

Youth Hostel and there is a large car park nearby.

Llanberis stands on the shore of Llyn Padarn at the foot of the Llanberis Pass and may be reached by rail from Caernarvon. It is the starting point of the Snowdon Railway, has several good hotels and guest houses, and there is a Youth Hostel on the mountainside above the town. It is the best centre for climbers making the long ascent to Yr Wyddfa by the well-trodden Llanberis Path, and also gives ready access to the frowning cliffs of Clogwyn Du'r Arddu.

Beddgelert spans the Afon Glaslyn at the junction of the main roads leading to Caernarvon, Portmadoc and Capel Curig and has several comfortable hotels and guest houses. The village is surrounded by the lower slopes of Snowdon and the southern satellites of Moel Siabod, while it is almost overshadowed by the fine peak of Moel Hebog. It is also within reasonable distance of Aberglaslyn Pass, and with the paths ascending the south side of Yr Wyddfa. The Nantlle Ridge is too far away for the average pedestrian, but may be reached by car or bus. Some four miles up the beautiful Vale of Gwynant stands the Youth Hostel of Bryn Gwynant, splendidly situated in a delightful sylvan setting overlooking the lake, while the guest house of the Holiday Fellowship is not far distant. Both are well placed for the ascent of Snowdon by the Watkin Path.

The Snowdon Ranger is now a Youth Hostel and is pleasantly situated on the shore of Llyn Cwellyn. The path to Yr Wyddfa, well known as the Snowdon Ranger, starts from its very door and may be the oldest route on this mountain. It is also well placed for access to the Nantlle Ridge and to Mynydd Mawr, which rises on the other side of the lake. It may be conveniently reached by bus from Caernarvon or Beddgelert.

Dolgellau, formerly known as Dolgelley, is centrally situated amid this vast area of peaks, which are so widely spread that those who stay here must use a car to reach them. It has one good hotel and there is a smaller one at Cross Foxes. The Youth Hostel of Kings is four miles away in the direction of Arthog and there is another at Pont ar Eden, Ganllwyd. The town is well placed for the ascent of Cadair Idris by the famous Foxes' Path, for the rock traverse of the shattered ridge of Cyfrwy, and also gives easy access to the Precipice and Torrent Walks, two of the scenic gems in this district.

Tal-y-llyn is the most romantically situated centre in Mid-Wales, and its two small but comfortable hotels stand at the foot of a sequestered lake that is completely enclosed by hills. It is the ideal starting point for the ascent of Cadair Idris by way of Cwm y Cau, one of the wildest in the Principality, and also for the ascent of the Pencoed Pillar, a nice problem for the rock climber.

Dinas Mawddwy has one hotel and is the only convenient centre for pedestrians wishing to make the most interesting ascent of the Arans. The key to this walk is the hamlet of Abercywarch, a mile to the north of the town, whence Cae Peris is reached by a narrow and twisting farm road giving access not only to the path to the two peaks but also to Craig Cywarch, a little-known crag of interest to the rock climber. There is a hut nearby.

Bala occupies a splendid position at the northern extremity of Llyn Tegid, but its hotels and guest houses are rather distant from the Arans and Arennigs, although strong walkers may attain the summits of either group in a long day. Those who can find accommodation in one of the cottages in Llanuwchllyn, a village at the southern extremity of Bala Lake, will be better placed for the ascents of both ranges and especially so for Aran Benllyn,

24

which is the nearer of the two.

Harlech is the nearest centre with adequate hotel accommodation and a Youth Hostel for those wishing to explore the Harlech Dome. It is a rugged backbone of bare mountains in the hinterland, in which the Roman Steps and the Rhinogs afford the toughest and most attractive climbing. Those having a car at their disposal may drive along the road to Barmouth and turn off to the left at Llanbedr, whence narrow and twisting lanes give access to one or other of the starting points that will be indicated later in this volume.

Llanbedr is a better centre for pedestrians undertaking the above expeditions, and there is a small hotel in the village.

Barmouth is an attractive seaside resort lying at the base of the southern slopes of the Harlech Dome, but is too far distant for the ascent of these peaks unless a car can be used for the long approach. The local scenic highlight is the famous Panorama Walk, which reveals fine views of the Mawddach Estuary below, backed by the precipitous front of Cadair Idris.

The Devil's Bridge is some twelve miles to the east of Aberystwyth and has a splendidly situated hotel overlooking the deep wooded stretches of the Rheidol Valley, from which it may be conveniently explored. It is a good though distant centre for the ascent of Plynlimon, when transport is desirable to reach the starting points of this walk. But pedestrians may secure accommodation at the Duffryn Castell Inn which lies at the foot of this immense sprawling mountain and the well-marked track to its summit is three and a half miles in length. Accommodation may also be found at Eisteddfa Gurig for the shorter route of ascent and there is a good hotel in Ponterwyd and a Youth Hostel at Ystumtuen.

Abergavenny has two hotels and is a convenient centre for motorists who wish to penetrate the deep valleys of the Black Mountains. Their bare, whaleback ridges afford excellent walking country some miles to the north of the town. There is a Youth Hostel at Capel-y-ffin.

Crickhowell also has two hotels, and some motorists may prefer to stay here for these pleasant drives. There is a Youth Hostel in the town.

Talgarth has one hotel and is the nearest town to the lofty Gadair Ridge which dominates the Black Mountains. Its crest may be most easily attained from the tiny adjacent hamlet of Pen-y-genffordd.

Hay lies in the Wye Valley to the north of the range and has two small hotels which are rather distant for the average pedestrian.

Brecon is the only centre with hotel accommodation near the Brecon Beacons, and a car is useful for those who wish to make the complete traverse of the lofty ridge that is dominated by Pen-y-Fan, the most picturesque peak in this range. There is a Youth Hostel at Ty'n-y-caeau, some two and a half miles to the east of the town.

Storey Arms is the nearest Youth Hostel to Pen y Fan and eight and a half miles from Brecon. It stands on the crest of the mountain road connecting this town with Merthyr Tydfil and may be reached from either by bus.

GLOSSARY OF WELSH PLACE-NAMES

READERS who do not speak the Welsh language may have some difficulty in understanding the various place-names given to the different topographical features of the Principality. I hope, therefore, the translation of some of them as set out below will be useful to travellers and climbers in this delectable country.

Aber, a river mouth.
Ach, water.
Aderyn, a bird.
Ael, a brow or edge.
Afon, a river.
Allt, a wooded slope.
Aran, a high place.
Arddu, a black crag.

Bach, little.
Bala, a lake outlet.
Ban, peak, crest, beacon.
Bedd, a grave.
Ber, a hilltop.
Bera ⎫
Bere ⎭ beak, top, point.
Betws, a chapel.
Beudy, a byre or cowhouse.
Blaen, the head of a valley.
Boch, a cheek.
Bod, a home or abode.
Bont, a bridge.
Braich, an arm or branch.
Bran, a crow.
Bras, thick or fat.
Brith, speckled.
Bron, the slope of a hill.

27

Brwynog, marshy.
Bryn, an eminence.
Bwlch, a pass.
Bychan, small.

Cadair, a chair or throne.
Cae, an enclosed field.
Caer, a camp or fortress.
Cafn, a trough.
Canol, middle.
Capel, a chapel.
Carn, a cairn or heap of stones.
Carnedd, a cairn.
Carreg, stone.
Caseg, a mare.
Castell, a castle or fortress.
Cau, a hollow.
Cefn, a ridge.
Celyn, holly.
Cidwm, a wolf.
Clogwyn, a cliff or precipice.
Clwyd, a gate.
Clyd, a shelter.
Cnicht, a knight.
Coch, red.
Coed, a wood.
Congl, a corner.
Cors, a bog or swamp.
Craig, a rock or crag.
Crib, a ridge or jagged edge.
Cribin, the small crest of a hill.
Croes, a cross.
Crug, a mound.
Cwm, a hollow or coombe.

Cwn, dogs.
Cymer, a confluence.

Dau, two.
Dinas, a natural fortress
Dol, a dale or meadow.
Drosgl, a rough hill.
Drum, a ridge.
Drws, a door.
Du or *ddu*, black.
Dwr, water.
Dyffryn, a wide valley.
Dysgl, a dish or plate.

Eglwys, a church.
Eigiau, a shoal of fish.
Eira, snow.
Erw, an acre.
Eryri, a highland.
Esgair, a shank or limb.

Fach, small.
Faes, a field or meadow.
Fan, peak, crest, beacon.
Fawr, large.
Felin, a mill.
Ffordd, a road.
Ffynnon, a well or fountain.
Foel, a bare or bald hill.
Fyny, upwards.

Gaer, a camp.
Gafr, a goat.
Gallt, a slope.
Ganol, middle.
Gardd, a garden.
Garn, an eminence.

Garth, an enclosure.
Gawr, a torrent.
Glas, blue-green.
Gludair, a heap.
Glyn, a deep valley.
Goch, red.
Golau, a light or beacon.
Golwg, a view.
Gors, a swamp.
Grach, scabby.
Groes, a cross.
Grug, heather.
Gwastad, a plain.
Gwern, an alder coppice.
Gwyn, white.
Gwynt, wind.

Hafod, a summer dwelling.
Hebog, a hawk.
Helgi, a hunting dog.
Helyg, willows.
Hen, old.
Heulog, sunny.
Hir, long.
Hydd, a stag.

Isaf, lower.

Las, blue-green.
Llan, a church.
Llech, a flat stone.
Llefn, smooth.
Llithrig, slippery.
Lloer, moon.
Llwyd, grey.
Llwyn, a grove.

Llyn, a lake.
Llys, a hall.
Lon, a lane.

Maen, a block of stone.
Maes, a field or meadow.
Man, a place.
Mawr, large.
Meirch, horses.
Melin, a mill.
Melyn, yellow.
Mign, a bog.
Min, lip or edge.
Mir, fair.
Moch, pigs.
Moel, a bare or bald hill.
Mor, sea.
Morfa, flat seashore—sea fen.
Mur, a wall.
Mynach, a monk.
Mynydd, a mountain.

Nant, a brook.
Newydd, new.

Oer, cold.
Og, harrow.
Ogof, a cave.
Oleu, light.
Onn, an ash tree.

Pair, a cauldron.
Pant, a hollow.
Parc, an enclosure.
Pen, a peak or top.
Penrhyn, a promontory.

Pentre, a village.
Perfedd, centre.
Perth, a hedgerow bush.
Pistyll, the spout of a water-
fall.
Plas, a mansion.
Poeth, hot.
Pont, a bridge.
Porth, a port, gateway.
Pwll, a pool.

Rhaeadr, a waterfall.
Rhiw, hill or slope.
Rhyd, a passage or ford.
Rhyn, a cape.

Saeth, an arrow.
Sarn, a causeway.
Silin, spawn.
Sych, dry.

Tal, end.
Tan, under.
Tir, soil.
Tomen, a mound.
Traeth, sandy shore.
Tref, a town.
Tri, three.
Trum, a ridge.
Twll, a cavern.
Twr, a tower.
Ty, a house.
Tyddyn, a small farmstead.

Uchaf, upper or higher
Un, one.

Waun, moorland.
Wen, white.
Wern, an alder swamp.
Wrach, a witch.
Wrth, near.

Y—Yr, the.
Yn, in.
Ynys, an island.
Ysfa, a sheep walk.
Ysgol, a ladder.
Ysgubor, a barn.
Ystrad, a street or dale.
Ystum, a curve or bend.
Ystwyth, winding.

THE WELSH PEAKS
52 ROUTES OF ASCENT

The Snowdon Group. Map 1

SNOWDON

1. Pen-y-pass and Crib Goch.
2. The Pyg Track.
3. The Miners' Track.
4. Lliwedd and Bwlch y Saethau.
5. The Watkin Path.
6. Yr Aran and Bwlch Main.
7. Rhyd-ddu and Llechog.
8. The Snowdon Ranger.
9. The Llanberis Path.
10. Cwm Glas.

2—TWP * *

The Glyders Group. Map 2

GLYDER FAWR

11. Ogwen Cottage and the Devil's Kitchen.
12. Cwm Idwal and the Nameless Cwm.
13. The Gribin.
14. Llyn Bochlwyd, Bristly Ridge and Glyder Fach.
15. Ogwen Cottage and Tryfan Scree Gully.
16. The North Ridge of Tryfan.
17. Heather Terrace.
18. Bwlch Caseg-fraith.
19. Gallt yr Ogof.
20. The Ridge from Capel Curig.
21. Pen-y-gwryd and the Miners' Track.
22. Pen-y-gwryd and Llyn Cwmffynnon.
23. Pen-y-pass and Esgair Felen.
24. Elidir Fawr from Deiniolen

Y GARN AND FOEL GOCH

25. Ogwen Cottage and Llyn Clyd.
26. Ogwen Cottage and the Devil's Kitchen.

The Carneddau. Maps 3 and 4

27. Llyn Crafnant and Clogwyn Mawr.
28. Creigiau Gleision.
29. Penllithrig-y-wrach.
30. Pen yr Helgi-du.
31. Helyg, Craig yr Ysfa and Carnedd Llywelyn.
32. Llyn Ogwen and Carnedd Ddafydd.
33. Ogwen Cottage and Pen yr Ole Wen.
34. Bethesda and Carnedd Llywelyn.
35. Aber Falls and Carnedd Llywelyn.

The Moel Siabod Group. Maps 5 and 6

36. The Royal Bridge and Moel Siabod.
37. Cyfyng Falls, Llyn y Foel and Moel Siabod.
38. Cnicht by the Dog Lakes.

39. Cnicht by Llyn Llagi.
40. Cnicht from Croesor.
41. The Moelwyns from Croesor.

The Moel Hebog Group. Map 7
42. Beddgelert and Moel Hebog.
43. The Nantlle Ridge.
44. Craig y Bere and Mynydd Mawr.

Cadair Idris. Map 8
45. Tal-y-llyn, Cwm y Cau and Pen y Gadair.

The Harlech Dome. Map 9
46. The Roman Steps and Rhinog Fawr.
47. Nant Col and Rhinog Fach.

The Arennigs. Map 10.
48. Bala, Llyn Arennig Fawr and Arennig Fawr.

The Arans. Map 11
49. Dinas Mawddwy and Drysgol.

Plynlimon. Map 12
50. From the Devil's Bridge.

The Black Mountains. Map 13
51. The Gadair Ridge.

The Brecon Beacons. Map 14
52. Cantref and Pen y Fan.

HEIGHTS OF THE PRINCIPAL WELSH PEAKS

(Arranged in order of altitude, in feet O.D. with their mountain group)

1.	3,560	Yr Wyddfa	. . .	Snowdon
2.	3,493	Crib Y Ddysgl, Carnedd Ugain	. . .	Snowdon
3.	3,484	Carnedd Llywelyn	.	Carneddau
4.	3,426	Carnedd Ddafydd .	.	Carneddau
5.	3,279	Glyder Fawr	.	Glyders
6.	3,262	Glyder Fach .	.	Glyders
7.	3,210	Pen yr Ole Wen	.	Carneddau
8.	3,195	Foel Grach	.	Carneddau
9.	3,152	Yr Elen	.	Carneddau
10.	3,104	Y Garn	.	Glyders
11.	3,091	Foel Fras	.	Carneddau
12.	3,029	Elidir Fawr	.	Glyders
13.	3,023	Crib Goch	.	Snowdon
14.	3,010	Tryfan .	.	Glyders
15.	2,970	Aran Fawddwy	.	Arans
16.	2,947	Y Lliwedd	.	Snowdon
17.	2,927	Pen y Cadair .	.	Cadair Idris
18.	2,907	Pen y Fan	.	Brecon Beacons
19.	2,901	Aran Benllyn	.	Arans
20.	2,875	Yr Aryg	.	Carneddau
21.	2,863	Corn Du	.	Brecon Beacons
22.	2,860	Moel Siabod	.	Moel Siabod
23.	2,804	Mynydd Moel	.	Cader Idris
24.	2,800	Arennig Fawr	.	Arennigs
25.	2,749	Llwytmor	.	Carneddau
26.	2,732	Pen yr Helgi-du	.	Carneddau
27.	2,726	Foel Goch	.	Glyders
28.	2,694	Carnedd y Filiast	.	Glyders
29.	2,664	Mynydd Perfedd	.	Glyders
30.	2,660	Waun Fach	. .	Black Mountains

31.	2,636	Nameless, E Llyn Caseg-fraith	.	Glyders
32.	2,624	Pen y Gadair Fawr	.	Black Mountains
33.	2,621	Penllithrig-y-wrach.	.	Carneddau
34.	2,608	Cribyn . . .	.	Brecon Beacons
35.	2,566	Moel Hebog . .	.	Moel Hebog
36.	2,564	Elidir Fach . .	.	Glyders
37.	2,557	Craig Cywarch	.	Arans
38.	2,528	Drum . . .	.	Carneddau
39.	2,527	Moelwyn Mawr	.	Moel Siabod
40.	2,499	Gallt yr Ogof	.	Glyders
41.	2,475	Y Llethr . .	.	Harlech Dome
42.	2,468	Pen Plynlimon Fawr	.	Plynlimon
43.	2,464	Diffwys . .	.	Harlech Dome
44.	2,451	Yr Aran . .	.	Snowdon
45.	2,451	Moel Llyfnant	.	Arennigs
46.	2,408	Craig Cwmsilyn	.	Nantlle Ridge
47.	2,397	Drysgol . .	.	Arans
48.	2,389	Craig Eigiau .	.	Carneddau
49.	2,382	Moel Eilio .	.	Snowdon
50.	2,362	Rhinog Fawr	.	Harlech Dome
51.	2,360	Pen Allt Mawr	.	Black Mountains
52.	2,334	Moelwyn Bach	.	Moel Siabod
53.	2,333	Rhinog Fach	.	Harlech Dome
54.	2,329	Trum y Ddysgl	.	Moel Hebog
55.	2,301	Carnedd Goch	.	Moel Hebog
56.	2,290	Mynydd Mawr	.	Moel Hebog
57.	2,287	Allt Fawr . .	.	Moel Siabod
58.	2,286	Y Garn II .	.	Nantlle Ridge
59.	2,265	Cnicht . .	.	Moel Siabod
60.	2,264	Arennig Fach	.	Arennigs
61.	2,214	Creigiau Gleision .	.	Carneddau
62.	2,207	Moel Cynghorion .	.	Snowdon
63.	2,167	Tyrau Mawr .	.	Cadair Idris
64.	2,152	Moel Druman	.	Moel Siabod
65.	2,148	Mynydd Talmignedd	.	Nantlle Ridge

66.	2,124	Moel yr Hydd	.	:	Moel Siabod
67.	2,094	Moel Lefn	.	.	Moel Hebog
68.	2,034	Pen y Castell	.	.	Carneddau
69.	2,032	Gallt y Wenallt	.	.	Snowdon
70.	2,020	Moel yr Ogof	.	.	Moel Hebog
71.	2,019	Gurn Wigau .	.	.	Carneddau
72.	2,000	Tal y Fan	.	.	Carneddau

THE PRINCIPAL WELSH LAKES

THIS list includes the more important Llynau viewed from the routes to the peaks. They are enumerated alphabetically under each mountain group, their height above O.D. is given in feet when known, together with their approximate situation.

SNOWDON

Bwlch Cwm-llan	—	Col between Yr Aran and Bwlch Main
Coch	1,705	Cwm Clogwyn
Du'r Arddu	1,901	Cwm Brwynog
Ffynnon-y-gwas	1,381	Cwm Clogwyn
Glas	—	Cwm Glas
Glas	—	Cwm Clogwyn
Glaslyn	1,971	Cwm Dyli
Gwynant	217	Vale of Gwynant
Llydaw	1,416	Cwm Dyli
Nadroedd	—	Cwm Clogwyn
Teyrn	1,237	Cwm Dyli

GLYDERS

Bochlwyd	1,806	Between Tryfan and Y Gribin
Caseg-fraith	—	Above Cwm Tryfan
Cwm-y-ffynnon	1,254	N. of Pen-y-pass

38

Y Cwn	—	Immediately S. of Devil's Kitchen
Idwal	1,223	Above Ogwen Cottage
Padarn	840	N. of Llanberis
Peris	840	E. of Llanberis

CARNEDDAU

Cowlyd	1,165	N. of Capel Curig
Crafnant	603	N.E. of Capel Curig
Dulyn	1,747	W. side of Cwm Eigiau
Eigiau	1,219	N. of Penllithrig-y-wrach
Ffynnon Lloer	—	N. of Llyn Ogwen
Ffynnon Llugwy	1,786	W. of Pen yr Helgi-du
Geirionydd	616	N. of Ugly House
Melynllyn	2,094	W. side of Cwm Eigiau
Ogwen	984	Crest of Nant Ffrancon

MOEL SIABOD

Yr Adar	1,874	N.E. of Cnicht
Y Biswail	—	N. end of Cnicht ridge
Croesor	—	N. of Moelwyn Mawr
Cwmcorsiog	—	N. of Llyn Croesor
Dinas	176	Vale of Gwynant
Diwaunedd	1,208	Below W. ridge of Moel Siabod
Edno	1,797	N. of Cnicht
Y Foel	1,756	Immediately E. of Moel Siabod
Llagi	1,238	Immediately W. of Llyn yr Adar
Lockwood	890	Pen-y-gwryd
Mymbyr	588	Capel Curig

MOEL HEBOG

Cwellyn	464	E. of Mynydd Mawr
Cwm Silin	1,105	W. end of Nantlle Ridge
Y Dywarchen	770	N.W. of Rhyd-ddu
Y Gader	598	S. of Rhyd-ddu
Nantlle Uchaf	322	W. end of Drws-y-coed Pass

CADAIR IDRIS

Y Cau	1,552	S. of Pen y Gader
Y Gadair	—	Immediately below Pen y Gader
Tal-y-llyn	270	S. of Dolgellau

HARLECH DOME

Arddyn	1,029	E. of Llawr Llech
Y Bi	—	S. of Rhinog Fach
Bodlyn	1,245	E. of Diffwys
Cwmbychan	605	Below the Roman Steps
Du	—	N. of Rhinog Fawr
Dulyn	—	S. of Y Llethr
Gloy	—	N. of Rhinog Fawr
Hywel	—	S. of Rhinog Fach
Morwynion	—	Bwlch Tyddiad
Perfeddau	—	N.W. of Y Llethr

THE ARENNIGS

Arennig Fawr	1,326	S.E. of Arennig Station

THE ARANS

Tegid Bala	530	N. of Aran Benllyn
Creiglyn Dyfi	—	Immediately E. of Aran Fawddwy

PLYNLIMON

Llygad Rheidol	—	Due N. of summit

BLACK MOUNTAINS

Grwyne Fawr	1,627	N.E. of Gader Ridge

BRECON BEACONS

Cwm-llwch	—	N.W. of Corn Du

MOUNTAIN PHOTOGRAPHY

I HAVE already written and lectured extensively on this fascinating branch of photography, and in my *Snowdon Holiday* I included copious notes on its application to the mountains of North Wales. But since this work has been out of print for some years, it may be useful to deal more fully with the subject herein than I did in its companion volume, *The Lakeland Peaks*. Moreover, I receive innumerable requests for tips from climbers who collect my works, and the following information may incidentally relieve me of much voluminous correspondence.

1. *The ideal camera for the mountaineer* is undoubtedly the modern miniature owing to its compact form, quick manipulation, great depth of focus, variety of lenses and thirty-six frames on each spool of film. While these instruments are represented in their best and most expensive type by the Leica, Contax and Nikon series, it does not follow that other less costly makes will not give good photographs. Recently I had the opportunity of making a comparative set of colour transparencies with the Leica and a camera that sells retail for about £12, and had I not been critical I should have been satisfied with the latter; for if you require a camera for your own pleasure and merely wish to show the prints or transparencies to your friends, they why pay over £100 for the instrument? In any case, I recommend that you consult your local dealer who will be happy to demonstrate the differences between the various makes and prices.

2. *The Lens* is the most important feature, and the best of them naturally facilitate the perfect rendering of the subject. A wide aperture is not essential, because it is seldom necessary to work out of doors at anything greater than F/4.5. It is advisable to use the objective at infinity in mountain photography because overall sharpness is then obtained, and to stop down where required to bring the

foreground into focus. It is in this connection that the cheaper camera, which of course is fitted with an inexpensive lens, falls short of its more costly competitors; for the latter are corrected for every known fault and the resulting photographs are then not only more acceptable for enlarged reproduction but also yield exhibition prints of superlative quality.

3. *A Lens Hood* is an indispensable accessory, because it cuts out adventitious light and increases the brilliance and clarity of the picture. Many climbers have the illusion that this gadget is only required when the sun is shining and that it is used to keep the direct rays out of the lens when facing the light source. While its use is then imperative, they overlook the fact that light is reflected from many points of the hemisphere around the optical axis, and it is the interception of this incidental light that is important.

4. *A Filter* is desirable, especially for the good rendering of skyscapes. A pale orange yields the most dramatic results, providing there are not vast areas of trees in the landscape in which all detail would be lost. It is safer to use a yellow filter, which does not suffer from this defect, and with autumn colours a green filter is very effective. *The Exposure Factors* do not differ materially, and in view of the wide latitude of modern black-and-white film the resulting slight differences in density can be corrected when printing. *For Colour Work* a skylight filter, formerly known as a Wratten 1A, is useful for reducing the intensity of the blues and for eliminating haze. This applies particularly to Kodachrome, but a filter is optional for this purpose when using Ilfochrome.

5. *Panchromatic Film* is to be preferred for landscapes, and the speed of modern types has been increased substantially, so much so that those having a Weston or ASA meter rating of up to 125 will yield grainless negatives providing they are processed with the developer that is recommended by the makers.

6. *Exposure and Development* are co-related. From May to September with bright sunlight and well-distributed clouds, films of the above speed require an average exposure of 1/250th of a second at an aperture of F/8 or 11 with a 2 × yellow filter, processed with a fine-grain developer for 7 minutes at a temperature of 68° F. Such negatives should be brilliantly clear and not too contrasty, and they will print on normal paper.

7. *The Best Time of Year* for photography among the Welsh Peaks is the month of May. A limpid atmosphere and fine cumulus are then a common occurrence and less time is wasted in waiting for suitable lighting. Colour work at this time is also satisfactory because the landscape still reveals the reds of the dead bracken, which, however, disappear in June with the rapid growth of the new fresh green fronds. Nevertheless, the most dramatic colour transparencies are obtained during the last week in October because the newly dead bracken is then a fiery red, the grass has turned to golden yellow, and the longer shadows increase the contrast between peak and valley.

8. *Lack of Sharpness* is a problem that causes disappointment to some amateurs, and they are often apt to blame the lens when the complaint is in fact due to camera shake. It is one thing to hold the instrument steady at ground level with a good stance and no strong wind to disturb the balance, while it is quite another problem in the boisterous breezes on the lofty ridges of Wales. When these conditions prevail, it is risky to use a lower speed than that indicated above, and maximum stability may be achieved by leaning against a slab of rock or in a terrific gale of wind by even lying down and jamming the elbows into the spaces between the crags; but foreground should never be sacrificed on this account. In calm weather a light tripod may be used, but in all other conditions it is too risky to erect one and have it blown over a precipice!

9. *Lighting* is the key to fine mountain photography, and

43

the sun at an angle of 45 degrees, over the left or right shoulder, will yield the required contrasts. These conditions usually appertain in the early morning or the late evening. If possible avoid exposures at midday with the sun overhead when the lighting is flat and uninteresting. Before starting on any climb, study the topography of your mountain so that full advantage can be taken of the lighting. Moreover, never be persuaded to discard your camera when setting out in bad weather, because the atmosphere in the hills is subject to the most sudden and unexpected changes, and sometimes wet mornings develop into fine afternoons, with magnificent clouds and limpid lighting. If your camera is then away back in your lodgings, you may live to regret the omission.

10. *The Sky* is often the saving feature in mountain photographs since cloudless conditions or a sunless landscape seldom yield a pleasing picture.

11. *Haze* is one of the bugbears in this branch of photography, and these conditions are especially prevalent among the Welsh Peaks during July and August. If an opalescent effect is desired, this is the time of year to secure it, but while such camera studies may be favoured by the purist, they seldom appeal to the climber who prefers to see the detail he knows exists in his subjects.

12. *Colour Photography* has been simplified in recent years by the introduction of cameras in which both exposure and aperture can be automatically adjusted to light conditions, and in consequence failures are rare. Owing to the narrow latitude of colour film correct exposure is essential if the resulting transparency is to approximate in hue to that of the landscape as seen by the eye. The only certain way to achieve success in all weather conditions is to *use a meter before making each exposure* and to be sure it is pointed at the same angle as the camera. This is most important, because if more sky is included in the meter than in the lens a shorter exposure will be indicated and this

will result in an under-exposed transparency in which the colour will be unduly intensified, whereas if the two operations are reversed it will be weakened. Excellent results are obtainable with Kodachrome and Ilfochrome, ASA 10, when an exposure of 1/50 second at an aperture of F/5.6 in sunlight between 10 a.m. and 4 p.m. during the summer months should produce satisfactory transparencies which may be viewed most advantageously by projection. However, *faster* colour film is now available, ASA 25 to 32, when an exposure of about 1/100 second at an aperture of F/8 yields superlative transparencies.

13. *Design or Composition* is the most outstanding feature of a good camera study; that is, one that not only immediately appeals to the eye, but rather one that can be lived with afterwards. Everything I have so far written herein on this subject comes within the scope of *Technique*, and anyone who is prepared to give it adequate study and practice should be able to produce a good negative, and from it a satisfying print.

But to create a picture that far transcends even the best snapshot requires more than this and might well be described as a flair, or if you like a seeing eye that immediately appreciates the artistic merits of a particular mountain scene. And strangely enough those who possess this rare gift usually produce a certain type of picture which is indelibly stamped with their personality; so much so that it is often possible to name the photographer as soon as his work is displayed. And, moreover, while this especial artistic trait may be developed after long application of the basic principles of composition, the fact remains that it is not the camera that really matters, for it is merely a tool, but the person behind the viewfinder, who, when satisfied with the design of his subject, ultimately and quite happily releases the shutter.

To the painter, composition is relatively easy, because he can make it conform to the basic principles of art by moving a tree to one side of his picture, or by completely removing a house from the foreground, or by inducing a stream to flow in another direction, or by accentuating the real subject, if it happens to be a mountain, by moving it or by increasing or decreasing its angles to suit his tastes. A photographer on the other hand has to move himself and his camera here and there in order to get these objects in the right position in his viewfinder. When he moves to one side to improve the position of one of them, another is thrown out of place, or perhaps the lighting is altered. In many cases, therefore, a compromise is the only solution, because if he spends too much time in solving his problem the mood may change, when his opportunity would be lost. It is just this element in mountain photography that brings it into line with sport, and, like golf, it can be both interesting and exasperating. Of course, the critic can sit in a comfortable chair by a warm fire at home and pull a photograph to pieces. He does not, perhaps, realise that the person taking the picture may have been wandering about knee-deep in a slimy bog, or that a bitterly cold wind was sweeping across a lofty ridge and making his teeth chatter, or that the light was failing, or that he had crawled out on a rocky spur with a hundred-foot drop on either side to get his subject properly composed.

Assuming, therefore, both lighting and cloudscape are favourable, what are the essential features of good composition? In the first place, you must select a pleasing object that is accented by tonal contrast as the centre of interest; in the second, you must place this object in the most attractive position in the frame or picture space; and in the third, you must choose a strong and appropriate foreground. Or, in other words, when the weather is favourable the success or failure of your photograph will depend entirely upon the *viewpoint*.

Thus, if your subject happens to be Snowdon, I may be able to help you with a few hints about five of the illustrations in this book. It is generally agreed that the eastern aspect of this mountain is the finest and it looks its best up to noon on a sunny morning with cloud drifting overhead. But you must first decide whether you wish to make a picture of the majestic peak itself, or of the whole range; if the former, there is one matchless viewpoint, whereas if the latter, there are at least three and each one of them has a different type of foreground.

Let us begin with the peak itself, whose tonal contrast will be enhanced by side lighting; whose strongest placing in a vertical frame will be in the centre of the picture space, as seen on the jacket of this book, and in a horizontal frame in the upper right-hand third as in plate 4; and whose most appropriate foreground will be Llyn Llydaw. Now, you must remember that it is always the foreground that leads the eye into a picture, and the treatment of the lake is therefore of the utmost importance. In the first place, the distant shore must never form a horizontal line above the lower third; for if you place it in the centre it will cut the picture into two halves. Moreover, some bold rocks on the near shore will add strength and interest to the whole study, and if you have a friend with you, ask him to stand near the shore to impart scale to the picture.

The beauty of the graceful lines of the Snowdon group always delights the eye and one of the nearest viewpoints that reveal them to advantage is Garth Bridge, above the little waterfall that enters the western end of Llynnau Mymbyr. The turbulent stream above the bridge, dappled with rocks and embellished by a single tree on the right, makes an excellent foreground for this photograph, as shown in plate 5. If you retreat farther from the range you will find another charming foreground in the Royal Bridge at the foot of Llynnau Mymbyr, but since Snowdon is now some ten miles distant its imposing character will be diminished if you do not use a long-focus lens. This allows the group to completely fill the frame and in your picture it

Plate 4. SNOWDON FROM LLYN LLYDAW

Plate 5. The Snowdon Group from Garth Bridge

Plate 6. Snowdon from the Royal Bridge, Capel Curig

Plate 7. Snowdon from the Pinnacles of Capel Curig

will assume a similar magnitude to that seen by the eye, as seen in plate 6. A higher viewpoint has certain advantages and you will find one by walking up to the Pinnacles of Capel Curig. From the lowest of them you will secure a splendid photograph in which the twin lakes and Plas-y-brenin yield a satisfactory foreground which leads the eye in one vast sweep to this magnificent mountain range, as shown in plate 7. Finally, whenever you take a shot of any of the Welsh Peaks, remember that it will be improved not only by placing a lake, a stream, a bridge, a figure or a group of climbers in the foreground, but also on occasion by introducing a tree or cottage or some object whose size if known will impart both interest and scale to your picture.

In conclusion, I would call your attention to the dramatic possibilities of photographing sunsets in colour; for by placing a still or slightly rippling lake in the foreground you will immensely enhance the whole picture by capturing the colour reflected by water as well as that already appearing in the sky.

PHOTOGRAPHY IN THE DIFFERENT GROUPS

I HAVE often been asked "What is the best view *of* such and such a mountain?" or "What is the most striking view *from* so and so?" These are difficult questions, because the answers depend so much upon one's personal tastes, which are influenced in no small degree by atmospheric conditions on any particular occasion. The present volume seems to be a convenient medium for an attempt to offer some guidance on this very debatable question, and while there are doubtless many who will disagree with my opinions, I shall give them for what they are worth. Where possible I have appended references to appropriate examples already portrayed in one or other of my works, as follows:

SL: *Snowdonia through the Lens*
SH: *Snowdon Holiday*
WW: *Wanderings in Wales*
EH: *Escape to the Hills*
WP: *The Welsh Peaks* (the present work)

The number indicates the plate in the particular volume, to which I have added the most suitable time of day for photographing the subject (G.M.T.). It should be noted that the examples given were not necessarily taken at the best time or season.

The suggestions are arranged according to the grouping system adopted throughout this work and under two headings: (1) The best pictorial views *of* the groups or their separate tops; (2) The most striking views *from* the groups. After what I have already written herein it will be obvious that foreground interest is of paramount importance since it bears a direct relationship to the pictorial rendering of the main subject.

THE BEST PICTORIAL VIEWS *of* THE GROUPS

The Eastern Aspect of Snowdon

    (*a*) From Llyn Llydaw before noon. SL 1; SH 52; EH 203; WP 4 & 18.

    (*b*) From Crib Goch before noon. SH 57; EH 208; WP 12.

    (*c*) From Garth Bridge before noon. WP 5.

    (*d*) From Llynnau Mymbyr any time of day. LS jacket; EH 1; EH 176.

    (*e*) From the Royal Bridge before noon. SL 5; EH 169; WP 6.

    (*f*) From the Pinnacles of Capel Curig before noon. WP 7.

The Western Aspect of Snowdon

    (*a*) From Y Garn II after 2 p.m. SH 43; WP 180 & 183.

    (*b*) From Craig y Bere and Mynydd Mawr after 2 p.m. WP 198.

The Northern Aspect of Snowdon
  (*a*) From the Glyders before noon. SL 34; WP 79.
  (*b*) From Llyn Padarn after 4 p.m. WP 55.
  (*c*) From Y Garn after 4 p.m. WP 106.

Crib Goch
  (*a*) From Pen-y-pass before 11 a.m. SL 51; EH 207.
  (*b*) From Crib y Ddysgl after 2 p.m. SL 53; WP 13.
  (*c*) From Cwm Glas after 3 p.m. SH 1; WP 62.

Lliwedd
  (*a*) From Llyn Llydaw before 10 a.m. SH 66.
  (*b*) From the Snowdon Horseshoe after 4 p.m. SH 68;
    EH 213; WP 11.

Yr Aran
  From Llyn Gwynant before 11 a.m. SL 42; WW 202;
  WP 33.

The Glyders
  From upper Nant Ffrancon after 4 p.m.

Tryfan
  (*a*) From Helyg before 11 a.m. SL 14; SH 76; Sunset
    SL 61; WP 85.
  (*b*) From Caseg-fraith Ridge before 11 a.m. SL 27;
    WP 1 & 86.

Bristly Ridge
  From Llyn Caseg-fraith before 11 a.m. SL 28; WW 188;
  EH 192; WP 89.

Cwm Idwal
  From Pen yr Ole Wen after 5 p.m. summer. SL 23; WP 144.

Y Garn
  From head of Llyn Ogwen before 11 a.m. WP 103.

Carneddau
  (*a*) From the Pinnacles of Capel Curig before noon.
    SL 12.
  (*b*) Craig yr Ysfa from Cwm Eigiau before 11 a.m.
    SH 7; WP 131.

(*c*) Black Ladders from Carnedd Ddafydd after 4 p.m. WP 140.

Moel Siabod

(*a*) From near the Ugly House before noon. SL 10.

(*b*) From the path to Llyn Crafnant before 11 a.m.

(*c*) From Clogwyn Mawr after 4 p.m.

Cnicht

From Tan Lan after 3 p.m. EH 187; SH 35; WP 157.

The Moelwyns

From the Afon Glaslyn after 3 p.m. WW 178; WP 170.

Moel Hebog

(*a*) From Llyn Dinas before noon. SL 44.

(*b*) From the Afon Glaslyn before noon. EH 198.

(*c*) From Pont Cae'r-gors after 5 p.m. SH 33.

(*d*) Y Garn II and Craig y Bere from Llyn y Gadair before 11 a.m. WP 181.

(*e*) Craig y Bere from Llyn y Dywarchen before noon. WP 195.

(*f*) Mynydd Mawr from the Snowdon Ranger before 11 a.m. WP 48.

(*g*) Mynydd Mawr from Waun-fawr after 3 p.m. WP 200.

Cadair Idris

(*a*) From the north after 5 p.m. summer. WW 104; WP 201.

(*b*) Craig y Cau from the east before 11 a.m. WW 106; WP 203.

(*c*) Pen y Gader from Cyfrwy after 3 p.m. WW 109; WP 207.

The Harlech Dome

(*a*) From the east before 11 a.m. WW 154; WP 209.

(*b*) Rhinog Fach from Llyn Hywel after noon. WW 161; WP 212.

The Arennigs

From the north-west after 4 p.m. WW 148.

The Arans
- (*a*) From Bala Lake after 5 p.m. WW 135.
- (*b*) Aran Benllyn from Drysgol before noon. WW 125; WP 219.

Plynlimon
- (*a*) From the south any time of day. WP 223.
- (*b*) From Eisteddfa Gurig before noon. WW 91; WP 226.

The Black Mountains
From Skirrid Fawr before 11 a.m. WW 24; WP 227.

The Brecon Beacons
- (*a*) From the main road to the east of Brecon before 11 a.m.
- (*b*) Pen y Fan from Cribyn before noon. WW 24; WP 233.

THE MOST STRIKING VIEWS *from* THE GROUPS

Snowdon
- (*a*) The Glyders and Crib Goch up to 3 p.m. SL 54; WP 14.
- (*b*) Lliwedd and Llyn Llydaw after 4 p.m. SH 65; WP 15.

Crib Goch
- (*a*) The Horseshoe before noon. SH 57; WP 12.
- (*b*) The Ridge and Pen y Pass up to 3 p.m. SH 61.
- (*c*) Llyn Glas and the Llanberis Lakes up to noon. SH 62.

Clogwyn Station
Llanberis Pass any time of day. WP 57.

Yr Aran
- (*a*) The South Ridge of Snowdon up to 2 p.m. WW 201; WP 34.
- (*b*) Moel Siabod and Llyn Gwynant about noon. WW 203; WP 37.
- (*c*) Mynydd Mawr and Llyn Cwellyn before noon. WW 204; WP 36.

The Glyders
- (a) Tryfan from Llyn Caseg-fraith before noon. WP 88.
- (b) Snowdon and the Castle of the Winds before 11 a.m. SL 43; WP 79.
- (c) The Devil's Kitchen from above after 4 p.m. SL 39; WP 102.
- (d) Cwm Glas from Esgair Felen after 4 p.m. SH 46; WP 98.
- (e) The Glyders from Y Garn after 2 p.m. WP 107.

Carneddau
- (a) Sunset from Carnedd Llywelyn, 5 p.m. onwards. SL 26; WP 135.
- (b) Snowdon and Cwm Idwal from Pen yr Ole Wen after 5 p.m. summer. WP 144.
- (c) Tryfan and Llyn Ogwen from Pen yr Ole Wen after 3 p.m. SL 24; WP 143.
- (d) Ogwen Valley from Clogwyn Mawr before noon. WP 114.
- (e) Llyn Crafnant from Clogwyn Mawr all day. SL 4; WP 113.

Moel Siabod
- (a) Western panorama comprising Hebog and Snowdon before noon. WP 153.
- (b) Cwm Dyli from Clogwyn Bwlch-y-maen in the morning.
- (c) Snowdon Horseshoe from Llyn Edno up to 2 p.m. SH 21; WP 159.
- (d) Snowdonia panorama from Cnicht any time of day. WP 161, 162 & 163.

Moel Hebog
- (a) Beddgelert and the Vale of Gwynant up to 3 p.m. SH 32; EH 197; WP 178.
- (b) Snowdon from Y Garn II after 2 p.m. SH 43; WP 180 & 183.
- (c) Snowdon from Craig y Bere after noon. WP 198.

(*d*) Nantlle Ridge from Craig Cwm Silin any time of day. WP 190.

Cadair Idris
    (*a*) Snowdon and the Harlech Dome from Cyfwry all day. WW 110; WP 205.
    (*b*) Mawddach Estuary from Cyfrwy all day. WW 111; WP 206.

The Harlech Dome
    (*a*) The Ridge from Rhinog Fawr after 2 p.m. WW 159; WP 210.
    (*b*) Y Llethr from above Llyn Hywel after 2 p.m. WW 163; WP 214.

The Arennigs
    Panorama of Snowdonia and Mid-Wales all day.

The Arans
    Cadair Idris from Aran Fawddwy before noon.

The Brecon Beacons
    (*a*) Corn Du from Pen y Fan in the morning. WW 36; WP 234.
    (*b*) Llyn Cwm-llwch from Corn Du in the morning. WW 37; WP 235.

NOTES ON THE ROUTES

I HAVE divided the Welsh Peaks into *twelve Mountain Groups* for the sake of convenience and easy reference. They commence with Snowdon because it is the highest mountain in the Principality and its ascent the most esteemed. The groups in this particular part of the region follow each other in clockwise sequence and end with the Moel Hebog range. *The Routes* to the dominating peak in each group are also arranged clockwise wherever possible so that they fit into the general scheme and thus avoid undue cross reference. This arrangement facilitates the choice of those routes which are more or less adjacent, as for instance the Rhyd-ddu Path and the Snowdon Ranger, where one of them can be ascended and the other descended. But I have purposely omitted any description of the *Descents* because when the ascents are reversed they obviously answer this requirement. *The Panorama* from the reigning peak in each group is always described at the termination of its first ascent. Many of the routes involve the traverse of subsidiary tops and the conspicuous features revealed from them are noted in passing, despite the fact that there may be a similarity in the views when the peaks are near together.

Farther south, however, I have not been able to follow this scheme because the ranges are more scattered. I have therefore first given details of Cadair Idris since it is the most popular peak and terminated the descriptions with that of Pen y Fan, in the Brecon Beacons, which is one of the most surprisingly beautiful mountains outside of Snowdonia.

Many of these attractive ranges have been sadly neglected by climbers, perhaps because they are less spectacular than those in North Wales. I have therefore described and illustrated only the route which discloses the finest topography in each group, but in many of them the terrain is relatively easy and other ways of reaching the summits may be worked out on the spot with little risk.

DISTANCES AND TIMES

THESE questions always involve a certain amount of speculation in mountaineering and I have purposely omitted any detailed reference to them in this work. *The Distances* may be calculated approximately from the maps, which are one inch to the mile, but it should be remembered that a map mile may in fact be considerably more than that owing to the undulating nature of the ground. *The Times* depend not only upon the pace and rhythm of each climber, but also upon the topography of the mountain as well as weather conditions. The best way to calculate them is to use the formula of Naismith, which allows one hour for each three map miles, plus half an hour for every 1,000 feet of ascent. This is fairly accurate for ordinary hill walking under favourable conditions, and while it includes reasonable halts for food and for viewing the grandeur of the mountain scene, it does not allow for bad weather, snow, rock climbing or photography, since the latter often involves much delay in finding the most effective foreground for any particular picture and for awaiting favourable lighting.

To make the application of this system clear, I will illustrate it by calculating the distance and time required for the complete circuit of the Snowdon Horseshoe, which is described and portrayed in my *Snowdon Holiday*, but may also be checked by combining Routes 1 and 4 noted in this volume.

It is three map miles from Pen y Pass to the summit of Snowdon by way of Crib Goch, and four miles back over Lliwedd and past Llyn Llydaw. This makes a total of seven map miles, which according to the above formula will take about two and a half hours. Since the starting point is at a height of 1,169 feet, this must be subtracted from the altitude of the first top, Crib Goch, 3,023 — 1,169 = 1,854 feet. Below this top lies Bwlch Coch on the 2,816-foot contour, and thence to Carnedd Ugain at 3,493 feet adds 677 feet to the ascent. Then again the point of emergence on the skyline of the zigzags is 3,258 feet, which makes a further addition of 302 feet to reach the summit of Snowdon at 3,560 feet—a total height climbed of 2,833 feet. But this is not the last rise in the Horseshoe; for after descending to Bwlch y Saethau at 2,691 feet, there is a further ascent of 256 feet to the cairn on Lliwedd at 2,947 feet. This makes a grand total of 3,089 feet, which according to the above formula adds one and a half hours, thus allowing altogether four hours for the complete traverse in favourable weather. However, as no account has been taken of halts for viewing the scenery from the four tops, or for food, and even if no time is spent in photography about one hour should be added, making five hours a reasonable time for fit and strong pedestrians to complete the whole circuit.

Since this book will be read by men and women of all ages, these figures may be discouraging to those in advancing years, and in these circumstances I think it will be useful, and perhaps indeed inspiring, to give the times taken on my last walk over this magnificent lofty ridge. On May 8th, 1956, I was in my sixty-fifth year and at 10 a.m. a young friend and I left Pen y Pass after a previous day of heavy rain. It was a cold, sunny, invigorating morning and we never hurried anywhere but reached Bwlch y Moch in an hour and Crib Goch at noon. We left the cairn half an hour later and stood on the summit of Snowdon at 2 p.m. where we spent a lazy hour in resting and refreshment. We passed the stony top of Lliwedd at 4 p.m. and were back at our starting point at 6 p.m., thus taking eight leisurely hours for this wonderful walk. I already possessed a good collection of photographs of the Horseshoe, but on this occasion took a further twenty-four shots in monochrome and a similar number in colour, all of which involved time spent in discovering unusual viewpoints. So, to those of you in the sixties and seventies, I say, Have a Go!

ROUTE FINDING IN MIST

IN these not uncommon conditions it is imperative to know with certainty your exact location on the map when the mist comes down to engulf you in gloom and to immediately note the direction to be taken. If you are on a well-cairned track no difficulties should be encountered, but when this is not the case you must estimate the distance to the next known point and set a course accurately by using your companion as a sighting mark. Keep him in view ahead while frequently referring to the compass and use your aneroid to check the rise and fall in the ground. If you are familiar with the gradient this will help to control your direction, but take nothing for granted; always trust the compass excepting when among magnetic rocks, basaltic and gabbro formations such as exist in the Coolins of Skye, and pay no attention whatsoever to gratuitous advice as to direction from compassless companions. Avoid contouring a slope; if you do this, you will no longer be master of your direction. It is always advisable to go straight down and never to diverge from a supposed obstacle without actual trial, because mist exaggerates both size and distance.

Should you be in the unhappy position of having no compass but *are familiar with the terrain* work your way down slowly over grass but never enter a ravine or gully or endeavour to descend a series of steep crags, whereas if you are on a ridge keep to its declining crest and if it forks make sure you take the known branch. If, on the other hand, you are alone on an uncairned track and also unfamiliar with the ground, stay put until the mist clears sufficiently for you to find your way. In these conditions you are in a very dangerous situation because mist sometimes persists for days in mountainous country. It is much better to practise map and compass reading in clear weather so that in mist you will have a reasonable chance of finding your way to safety.

ACCIDENT PROCEDURE

DISTRESS SIGNAL. *Six* long flashes or *six* long blasts of a whistle in quick succession followed by a pause of one minute. This is repeated again and again until assistance is forthcoming.

THE REPLY to this signal is in a similar vein; that is *three* flashes or blasts of a whistle followed by a pause of one minute, repeated again and again.

BROCKEN SPECTRES

THESE remarkable phenomena are confined to hill country, and in consequence may, with luck, be observed by any climber on the Welsh Peaks, especially if he happens to be on a ridge enclosing a cwm filled with mist. They appear as gigantic shadows seen on the surface of the mist and were first observed on the Brocken in Germany, hence the name, but are said to be an optical illusion because the shadow is quite close and of actual size. It is usually only possible for each climber to see his own spectre.

GLORIES

THESE appear as a coloured ring round the shadow cast by the climber on the mist in similar circumstances. Each member of a climbing party can see only his own glory.

THE SNOWDON GROUP

YR WYDDFA . . .	3,560 feet
CRIB Y DDYSGL . . .	3,493 feet
BWLCH GLAS (ZIGZAGS) .	3,258 feet
CRIB GOCH . . .	3,023 feet
Y LLIWEDD . . .	2,947 feet
BWLCH COCH . . .	2,816 feet
BWLCH Y SAETHAU . .	2,691 feet
YR ARAN	2,451 feet
MOEL EILIO . . .	2,382 feet
MOEL CYNGHORION . .	2,207 feet
GALLT Y WENALLT . .	2,032 feet
BWLCH Y MOCH . . .	1,925 feet
BWLCH CWMBRWYNOG .	1,625 feet

MAP 1
THE SNOWDON GROUP

IT is only right and proper that Snowdon should assume pride of place in the following pages, not so much because it is the dominating peak of Wales, but more especially as its elevation is perhaps the finest in the Principality and most of the routes to its summit admit of little variation. All of them are clearly defined throughout and five traverse lofty ridges for part of the way.

It is scarcely surprising that the most popular starting point is Pen y Pass, since Routes 1 and 4 together form the famous Horseshoe, a ridge "walk" that is full of interest all the way and reveals the mountain at its best. The fact that Pen y Pass stands on the 1,169-foot contour may mislead some climbers into supposing that the actual ascent is therefore reduced to less than 2,400 feet, but as I have shown in the monograph on *Distances and Times* this is really 2,833 feet owing to the undulations of the ridge. In view of this fact there is not much difference in the height to be climbed from some of the other starting points, such as Llyn Cwellyn, which involves about 3,000 feet, and Llanberis, 3,200 feet. The lowest point of departure is the Vale of Gwynant at about 200 feet and as the Watkin Path rises continuously it involves over 3,300 feet of ascent. But against these differences in altitude must be placed the length of the walk which from Pen y Pass is about three map miles, from Llyn Cwellyn and the Vale of Gwynant a little more and from Llanberis about five map miles. Then again the gradient has to be considered, and while the Llanberis Path is usually regarded as the easiest, those of the Snowdon Ranger and Watkin Path are a little harder, and that from Pen y Pass by way of Crib Goch is the steepest of them all.

All the routes described and illustrated herein are so well trodden that even in misty weather they should present no great difficulties, whereas in snow and mist they should be left severely alone, and especially so if snow lies on ice as this treacherous condition is often the cause of accidents in the most unsuspected places.

Plate 8. PEN Y PASS. STARTING POINT OF ROUTES 1, 2, 3, 4 AND 10

SNOWDON

Route 1. Pen y Pass and Crib Goch. Leave the car park below the crest of the Llanberis Pass and follow the higher track which starts under the double electricity pole, as waymarked; it rises along the northern flanks of the Last Nail in the Horseshoe right up to Bwlch y Moch. For the first few hundred yards the route mounts over boulders and those climbers wearing Vibrams should be careful here as they are usually very slippery after rain. The path then meanders over grass and boggy ground and after passing through a collection of gigantic boulders it swings round to a derelict sheepfold at the base of some crags. This is the junction for the rather indistinct path over to the right which eventually leads into Cwm Glas. Ahead rises the broad, stony track to Bwlch y Moch, with Crib Goch towering overhead all the way. On attaining the pass the route forks; the left branch is the Pyg Track and the right branch our route to Crib Goch. At this point there is a fine view into Cwm Dyli, with Lliwedd on its far side and Llyn Llydaw below. Our well-trodden path now steepens and while gaining height winds in and out of several rocky outcrops until, with the disappearance of grass, it begins to rise sharply. Ahead there is one tricky bit that is almost vertical, but a reliable hand-hold, high up on the right, gives sufficient pull to pass this hazard safely. Beyond it nail marks lead upwards to the rocky staircase which eventually emerges by the cairn on our first summit.

The spacious prospect from Crib Goch is electrifying in its magnificence; for ahead the narrow rock ridge undulates as far as the Pinnacles which are crowned by the noble cone of Yr Wyddfa. To the L. of the reigning peak the ridge falls to Bwlch y Saethau and then rises again to Lliwedd whose cliffs descend steeply to Llyn Llydaw far below. To the R., and beyond the Pinnacles, the ridge rises in steps from Bwlch Coch to Crib y Ddysgl, with the zigzags on its L.

68

Last Nail in the Horseshoe

Bwlch y Moch

Snowdon

Crib Goch

Cwm Glas

Llanberis Pass

Pen y Pass

Plate 9. ROUTES 1, 2, AND 10

Crib Goch →

Snowdon →

Bwlch y Saethau →

Bwlch Moch →

Pyg Track

Plate 10. ROUTES 1 AND 2

Lliwedd

Llyn Llydaw

Miners' Track

Plate 11. THE VIEW FROM BWLCH Y MOCH ON ROUTES 1 AND 2

and the Parson's Nose below on its R. Farther to the R. there is a bird's-eye view into Cwm Glas, with its tiny lake cupped in the base of the hollow, and beyond it a distant view of the Llanberis Lakes. Still farther to the R. rise the chain of the Glyders, separated from this lofty perch by the deep Llanberis Pass, whose road may be perceived as a thin white line far below.

Some 400 yards of knife-edge leads to the Pinnacles, but those with a steady head will experience no difficulties in crossing it in calm weather. These obstacles may be traversed by means of ample hand- and foot-holds, but those who prefer to avoid them may pass to the left and regain the track lower down. Bwlch Coch is soon encountered, with views on the L. of Glaslyn at the foot of Yr Wyddfa, whence the track rises along the crest of the ridge, ascends an easy chimney on the R., and emerges immediately below Crib y Ddysgl. There are several paths on this broad shoulder, but do not take the one on the right because it leads to the top of the Parson's Nose, a cliff only suitable for experienced rock climbers. Beyond the summit of Carnedd Ugain the track descends gently and swings round to the left to Bwlch Glas, at the exit of the zigzags, and here the railway is encountered and followed to the summit of Snowdon.

On a clear day the immense panorama unfolded from the large cairn on Snowdon is one of the finest in Britain, and despite the fact that it is possible to pick out the coast of Eire, the Isle of Man and Scafell Pike, in Lakeland, these objects are too far away to hold the gaze of the climber, and unconsciously his eye is drawn to the more attractive and closer detail of the landscape in the shape of the spurs of Snowdon itself. Of these, it is perhaps the sheer cliffs of Lliwedd that first attract his eye, but since the sun is always on the wrong side of this peak for its full appraisal, it is only natural to turn to the ridge he has just traversed enclosing the blue-green waters of Glaslyn far below. It

Snowdon Bwlch Glas Crib y Ddysgl

← Zig–Zags

Bwlch Coch

To Cwm Glas

Crib Goch

Plate 12. ROUTE 1—THE SNOWDON HORSESHOE FROM CRIB GOCH

may well be that Crib Goch will rivet his attention by reason of its diminutive appearance, as it looks a long way below although there is a difference in altitude of barely 600 feet. Beyond the ridge rising to Crib y Ddysgl the solitudes of the Glyders appear tremendous and beyond them again there is a glimpse of Carnedd Llywelyn and Pen yr Ole Wen. To the east the twin Capel Lakes catch the light at the foot of Moel Siabod, and on swinging round to the south the cliffs of Cadair Idris stand out on the far horizon. Nearer at hand and in the south-west Moel Hebog is prominent, and the ridges of this group trail away to the north to end with the bold and compact form of Mynydd Mawr. The circle is completed with the glint of light on Llyn Cwellyn, R. of which Moel Eilio leads the eye to the flat expanse of Anglesey and the sea.

It is always inspiring to stand on the highest peak south of the border and to scan the vast scenes described above, with the ground falling away at one's feet, but I never experience the same thrill here as I do on Crib Goch. On the latter I have the impression of complete detachment, coupled with the prospect of a higher peak ahead which has still to be conquered—and I look up. Here, however, on Yr Wyddfa, the peak has been won, the pendant ridges fall away—and I look down. Moreover, there is the constant reminder of other human beings, augmented during the summer season by the crowds that have not come up the hard way, and if you feel as I do, dear reader, walk over the Snowdon Horseshoe on a sunny day in early spring or late autumn when the profound solitude of this lofty ridge will act as balm to your soul.

Moel Siabod

Pinnacles

Bwlch Coch

Crib Goch

Lynnau Mymbyr

Llyn
Cwmffynnon

To Snowdon

Plate 13. Route 1 The Paths on Crib y Ddysgl

Pen yr Ole Wen → | Carnedd Llywelyn | Glyders | Crib Goch | Llyn Llydaw

Pyg Track → | Snowdon

Plate 14. ROUTE 1—NORTH-EAST FROM SNOWDON

Lliwedd

Watkin Path

Bwlch y Saethau

Llyn Llydaw

Miners' Track

Plate 15. Route 1—South-east from Snowdon

SNOWDON

Route 2. The Pyg Track. Follow Route 1 as far as Bwlch y Moch where the path forks and take the left branch which undulates slightly across the southern flanks of Crib Goch. It is well cairned throughout and one of the most popular routes to Snowdon, and, moreover, it has the advantage of disclosing on the L. one of the most dynamic views of the majestic cliffs of Lliwedd beyond Llyn Llydaw. Yr Wyddfa towers into the sky ahead until a prominent cairn is reached above Glaslyn and it reveals this blue lake below at the foot of its precipices. At this point the track goes to the R. and is soon joined by the Miners' Track coming up from this lake, whence the rough and steep ascent of the zig-zags lead to the skyline at Bwlch Glas, where Route 1 is joined and followed to the summit of the reigning peak.

Snowdon

Bwlch Glas and Zig-Zags →

Bwlch y Saethau →

Cribin →

Glaslyn →

Pyg Track

Plate 16. ROUTE 2

SNOWDON

Route 3. The Miners' Track. Leave the car park at Pen y Pass by the old road leading to the Copper Mines. It is rough and stony, but rises at a gentle gradient with views on L. of Moel Siabod and the sylvan Vale of Gwynant. It contours round the south-eastern slopes of the Last Nail in the Horseshoe, and at a sharp turn to R. reveals Lliwedd, Snowdon and Crib Goch towering ahead. The route now takes a direct line for the peaks and passes round and above Llyn Teyrn on L., whose shore is marred by derelict buildings, and thereafter bears R. until Llyn Llydaw is reached. This is a superb viewpoint because it unveils one of the classic and most majestic prospects of Yr Wyddfa, while on L. of it there is also a good view of Lliwedd. Keeping the lake on L., the broad track crosses its lower end by a causeway, which may be under water when the lake is full and then necessitates a detour to the R. The path winds along the shore of Llyn Llydaw, passes some unsightly and derelict mine buildings, and then turns sharp R. when the first considerable rise is encountered. The path mounts on R. of the stream coming down from Glaslyn, with Yr Wyddfa towering into the sky ahead, and later reaches the outflow of this sombre lake. Thence the level path rims its north shore, passes mine workings which should be avoided and more derelict buildings, until a steep scree track on R. rises to join the Pyg Track, when Route 2 is followed to the summit of Snowdon.

Plate 17. ROUTES 2 AND 3 ASCEND THE ZIG-ZAGS

← Lliwedd

Bwlch y
Saethau

Snowdon →

Bwlch Glas →

Miners' Track →

Plate 18. Route 3—Snowdon from Llyn Llydaw

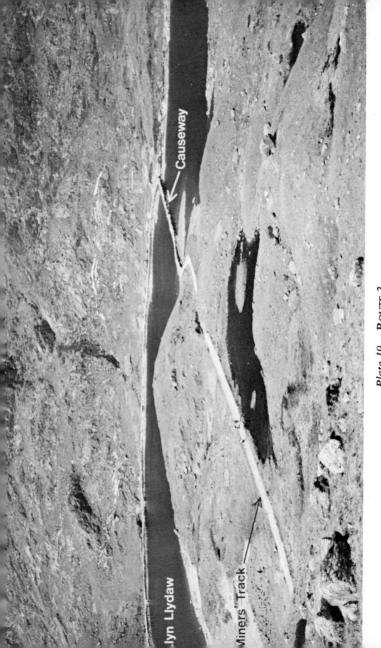

Plate 19. ROUTE 3

Plate 20. ROUTE 3

Bach Lliwedd East Peak West Peak

Llyn Llydaw

Miners' Track

Snowdon

Miners' Track

Plate 21. ROUTE 3

SNOWDON

Route 4. Lliwedd and Bwlch y Saethau. Follow Route 3 to Llyn Llydaw and bear L. on reaching the lake. The track rises gently at first, but do not take the rather indistinct branch on the R. at the fork because this is used by rock climbers making for the cliffs of Lliwedd. Thence the path deteriorates and becomes very rough as it rises steeply to the col between Gallt y Wenallt on the L. and Lliwedd Bach on the R. There is a prominent cairn on the ridge that is a useful landmark in mist. Now turn R. and keep to the crest of the ridge, with sensational drops on the R., first over the lesser eminence of Lliwedd Bach and thereafter over the East Peak of Lliwedd, where the precipices on the R. disappear into space, with Llyn Llydaw far below. There is a slight fall to the little col ahead and then a rise to the West Peak of Lliwedd, where the grand retrospect is worthy of attention as it is one of the most dramatic scenes on the Horseshoe. Still keeping to the edge of the cliffs, the well-marked track descends over tricky rock and boulders, and care is needed here as a slip on the R. would be fatal. The path levels out on the approach to Bwlch y Saethau and is joined by the Watkin Path coming up on the L. from Cwm-llan. The last section, rising diagonally over scree to Y Wyddfa, is the most trying part of this ascent, and while this most used track slants to the L. across the shattered flanks of the peak, many climbers prefer to make a direct attack upon it and emerge on the skyline on the east shoulder of Snowdon below the cairn.

Snowdon

Glaslyn

Miners' Track

Plate 22. ROUTE 3

Zig-Zags

Pyg Track

Miners' Track

Miners' Track

Glaslyn

Plate 23.   ROUTES 2 AND 3

Bwlch y Saethau

Gribin Ridge →

Lliwedd →

Glaslyn

Plate 24. THIS SCENE IS PASSED ON L. OF ROUTE 3

Plate 25. ROUTE 4

Bach   E   &   W Peaks of Lliwedd

To Snowdon →

Llyn Llydaw

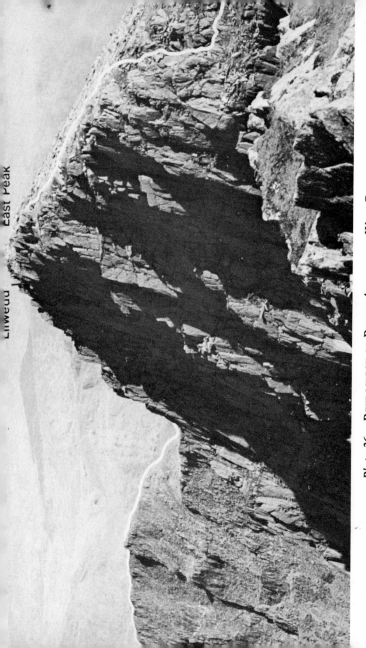

Lliwedd East Peak

Plate 26. RETROSPECT OF ROUTE 4 FROM THE WEST PEAK

SNOWDON

Route 5. The Watkin Path. This popular ascent leaves the main road threading Nant Gwynant opposite the car park at Pont Bethania. A gate gives access to the resurfaced road leading to Hafod-llan farm, but after some 500 yards it bears L. through the rhododendrons along the old miners' road and emerges above the stream coming down from Cwm y Llan. A charming waterfall is passed on the R. and above it an almost level stretch passes some derelict mine buildings on R., goes over a wooden bridge to Plas Cwm-llan also on R., and with a view high up on the L. of the summit of Yr Aran. This one-time pleasant residence was used during the Second World War as a target for Commandos and is now an unsightly ruin. Thence the track passes close to the Gladstone Rock on L., where a tablet commemorates the opening of this path by Gladstone, then eighty-four years of age, on September 13th, 1892. The yawning mouth of Cwm-llan now opens up ahead and is entered by a shaly path leading to a deserted slate quarry, but turn sharp R. before reaching the roofless buildings and climb steadily with Bwlch Main towering on L. and Craig Ddu rising on R. A little rock gateway appears on the skyline ahead and this reveals the most shattered front of Snowdon, whence the path meanders round to the R. and ultimately joins Route 4 on the crest of Bwlch y Saethau. The view from this pass comes as a surprise; for it discloses Glaslyn below on L. and the full length of Llyn Llydaw on R., between which a rough rock spur, known as Y Gribin, affords a nice scramble for those wishing to reach Route 3.

Plate 27. ROUTE 5

Plate 28.   Route 5—The Watkin Path Starts Here

Lliwedd

Snowdon

Craig Ddu

Bwlch Main

To Snowdon

Plate 29. ROUTE 5—THE RUINS OF PLAS CWM-LLAN

Yr Aran

To Snowdon

Gladstone Rock

Plate 30. ROUTES 5 AND 6

Plate 31. ROUTE 5—TABLET ON GLADSTONE ROCK

Plate 32. THE TERMINAL STRETCHES OF ROUTE 5

Lliwedd

Watkin Path

Snowdon

Yr Aran →

Plate 33. Route 6—Yr Aran from Llyn Gwynant

Route 6. Yr Aran and Bwlch Main. Follow Route 5 to Plas-cwm-y-Llan and then turn L. and begin the grassy, trackless ascent of the eastern shoulder of Yr Aran. The cairn soon appears on the skyline and is easily attained; it opens up splendid prospects in all directions; with a fine vista to the north-west of Mynydd Mawr and Llyn Cwellyn, and a grand view to the north-east of Moel Siabod, with a glimpse of Llyn Gwynant below. But the magnificent perspective of the South Ridge of Snowdon will rivet the gaze and its crest affords the final section of this route to Yr Wyddfa. There is at first a sharp descent to Bwlch Cwm-llan, where a rock-bound pool on the R. and an almost round little tarn on the L. will charm the eye. Thereafter the collar work begins: keep to the edge of the sharp drops on R. and on attaining the saddle the Rhyd-ddu Path comes in on the L. from Llechog, whence ascend the clearly marked track along the crest of Bwlch Main to attain the cairn on the summit of the peak.

Plate 34. ROUTE 6

Craig Cwm Silyn   Nantlle Hills   Y Garn II

Llyn y Gadair

Plate 35.   Route 6—South-west from Yr Aran

Craig y Bere →   Mynydd Mawr →   Llyn Cwellyn   Foel Goch →

Plate 36. ROUTE 6—WEST FROM YR ARAN

← Moel Siabod

Llyn Gwynant →

Cwm y Llan →

Yr Aran

Plate 37. ROUTE 6—NORTH-EAST FROM YR ARAN

← Snowdon

Plate 38. BWLCH MAIN. FINAL STRETCH OF ROUTES 6 AND 7

Pitt's Head →   Moel Hebog ↓

Plate 39. KEY TO ROUTE 7

SNOWDON

Route 7. Rhyd-ddu and Llechog. This easy ascent is one of the neglected delights of the group and incidentally most rewarding to photographers. There are two starting points: that nearest Beddgelert is favoured by pedestrians and the other, just outside the hamlet of Rhyd-ddu, is preferred by motorists because South Snowdon Station, on the long-disused Welsh Highland Railway, has been converted into a spacious car park and is quite close to the gate giving access to the main route. The key to the former is Pitt's Head on the Beddgelert–Caernarvon road. Turn R. here for the sequestered farm of Ffridd-uchaf, easily recognised by its embowering shield of conifers; pass it on L. and follow the grassy track until it merges with the quarry road coming up from Rhyd-ddu. The key to the latter is an iron gate from which the disused quarry road goes due east. Pass a deep quarry on R., conspicuous by the V-shaped opening in its far wall, and follow the road as it contours round the hillside until some bold rocks are encountered on L. This is a splendid viewpoint for the appraisal of Llyn Cwellyn, enclosed on L. by Mynydd Mawr and on R.

The Saddle

Snowdon

Llechog

Ffriod Uchaf

Pitt's Head

Plate 40. START OF ROUTE 7—WALKERS FROM BEDDGELERT

by Foel Goch. A few steps ahead pass through another gate and on the face of the crag opposite directions are given for the next turn in the track which otherwise might be missed. This is an iron gate on L. situated at the point of mergence with the Beddgelert track. The route now takes a direct line for Llechog, well seen on the skyline with Yr Wyddfa on R., and it winds its way uphill in and out of rocky outcrops, eventually to reach another gate in a substantial stone wall, with a large sheepfold on the other side. This is a good near-viewpoint for Yr Aran, and also for the many tops of the Moel Hebog range in the distant southwest. The path is unmistakable and soon crosses a level green clearing containing the ruin of a hut, long ago used as a place of refreshment, after which it rises more steeply over rock and scree ultimately to thread the boulders scattered in profusion on the broad crest of Llechog. This is a revealing coign of vantage, since its steep slabs fall into the vast basin of Cwm Clogwyn, embellished by several twinkling tarns, and on R. to the conspicuous shoulder and serrated ridge of Bwlch Main. Farther to the R. there is a grand array of the peaks crowning the Moel Hebog group, below which Llyn y Gadair and Llyn Cwellyn reflect the afternoon light. Now climb the broad stony track to the saddle and here join Route 6 for the summit of Snowdon, meanwhile enjoying the enchanting views on R. of Cwm-llan and of Moel Siabod above Bwlch y Saethau.

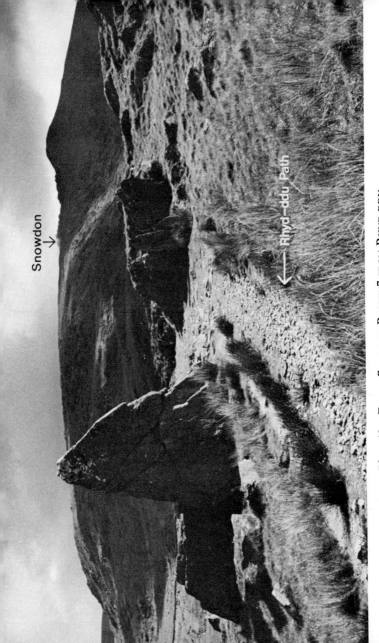

Snowdon →

Rhyd–ddu Path

Plate 41. EARLY STAGE OF ROUTE 7 FROM RHYD-DDU

Plate 42. ROUTE 7

Snowdon   ← Saddle

Llechog →

Ffriod Uchaf

Rhyd-ddu →

Plate 43. ROUTE 7—SEEN FROM THE POINT WHERE THE TWO TRACKS MERGE

Moel Eilio →

← Mynydd Mawr

Craig y Bere →

Cwm Clogwyn

Llechog

Track to Snowdon

Plate 44. RETROSPECT FROM ROUTE 7

Snowdon Bwlch Main Saddle

Cwm Clogwyn

Llechog

Plate 45. ROUTE 7

Plate 46. BACKWARD VIEW OF ROUTE 7

Llyn Nantlle Uchaf

Llyn Cwellyn

Llyn y Dywarchen

Llechog

Cwm Clogwyn

← Llyn y Gadair

Rhyd—ddu

Saddle

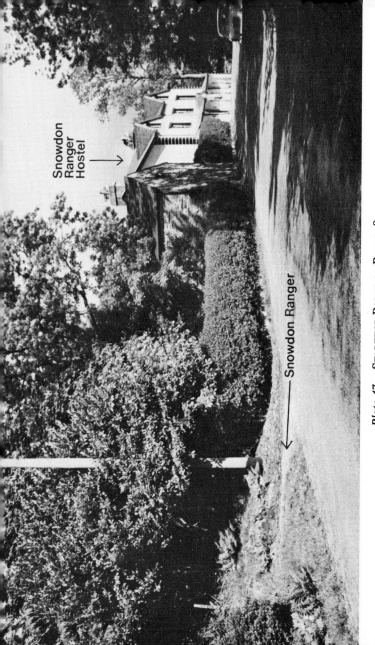

Snowdon Ranger Hostel

Snowdon Ranger

Plate 47. STARTING POINT OF ROUTE 8

SNOWDON

Route 8. The Snowdon Ranger. This may well be the oldest route to Snowdon and is named after its first guide who may have lived in or near the present Youth Hostel which faces the rippling waters of Llyn Cwellyn. It yields a very pleasant approach to Yr Wyddfa and is seldom crowded, save on those rare occasions when the ardent youth hostellers invade it in force. Start the ascent by passing through a gate to the L. of the Hostel and make for the farm farther up the green hillside. Then zigzag through the pastures above it and go through a gate in a stone wall on top R. This gives access to a wide grassy path, with a wonderful retrospect of Mynydd Mawr and Llyn Cwellyn, and farther on of the Nantlle Ridge and Moel Hebog. Go through a small iron gate, round which sheep often congregate, and then tread the gradually rising moorland path, with a grand prospect ahead of Cwm Clogwyn, enclosed on L. by the slopes of Clogwyn Du'r Arddu, on the R. by the cliffs of Llechog, and dominated by Yr Wyddfa.

The well-trodden path passes below Bwlch Cwm-brwynog, but walk up to it on L. and rest awhile to enjoy the fine retrospect of the Moel Hebog range on the other side of the valley. Then, instead of rejoining the path on R., keep to the crest of Clogwyn Du'r Arddu, and from a safe viewpoint look down its beetling precipices, which are the playground of the expert rock climber, to the stygian waters of Llyn Du'r Arddu, cradled in a wilderness of boulders at the foot of the crags. From the top of this eminence note the view of the Snowdon Railway near Clogwyn Station, backed by the shapely tops of the Glyders. Thereafter, return to the track on R. and follow it to the summit of Snowdon, of which the section below the fork comes up from Llanberis.

Note.—An alternative approach starts at Bron Fedw Isaf and is waymarked to join the original track higher up the hillside.

Mynydd Mawr →   Craig Cwm–bychan →

Llyn Cwellyn

YH ↗

Plate 48. RETROSPECT FROM ROUTE 8

Plate 49. VIEW R. OF ROUTE 8

Nantlle Ridge

Llyn Cwellyn

Moel Hebog →

← Llyn y Gadair

Plate 50. VIEW AHEAD OF ROUTE 8

Clogwyn Du'r Arddu

Snowdon

Llechog

Cwm Clogwyn

Plate 51. ROUTE 8

Snowdon →

Clogwyn Du'r Arddu →

Plate 52. ROUTE 8—POINT OF DIVERGENCE

Llyn Padarn and Llanberis

Llyn Du'r Arddu

Clogwyn Du'r Arddu

Plate 53. BIRD'S-EYE VIEW OF LLYN DU'R ARDDU FROM ROUTE 8

Plate 54. FINAL STRETCH OF ROUTE 8, SEEN FROM CLOGWYN DU'R ARDDU

Route 9. The Llanberis Path. This is the longest, least arduous and most popular route to Snowdon; it involves a walk of about five miles over a gently graded path and at the Halfway House refreshments are obtainable, a boon much appreciated by climbers on a hot summer day. The key to this route is the Square at the end of the first side road above the Snowdon Railway Station, where a gate gives access to a mounting by-road, with the railway on R. This degenerates into a rough stony path, which may be rather damp after a wet spell, and on turning L. it continues to rise, passes under the railway, and then levels out right up to the Halfway House. The majestic cliffs of Clogwyn Du'r Arddu are now revealed and they appear on R. until the path rises above them after passing Clogwyn Station. Hereabouts is the real reward of the ascent; for by going over to the spur nearby the most dramatic view is obtained of the Llanberis Pass, far below and hemmed in by the steep slopes of Snowdon and the Glyders. Continuing the ascent, the path goes under the railway and keeps beside it and below the dome of Crib y Ddysgl, all the way to the end of the line, whence the large cairn just above the hotel crowning Yr Wyddfa is quickly attained.

Esgair Felen

Llanberis Pass

Crib Goch

Snowdon

Plate 55. Distant View of Route 9 from Llyn Padarn

Half Way House ←

Llanberis Path →

Plate 56. RAILWAY AND ROUTE 9 RUN SIDE BY SIDE

Glyder Fawr

Moel Siabod →

Plate 57. LLANBERIS PASS, SEEN FROM CLOGWYN STATION

Plate 58. ROUTE 9

SNOWDON

Route 10. Cwm Glas. This sporting route is seldom used, save by the connoisseur who can revel in the solitude and wild grandeur of Cwm Glas, which is decked with Alpine flora in the spring and graced by a lovely tarn that opens up a surprising view of the Glyders. Follow Route 1 to the sheepfold and then bear R. over a grassy shoulder to a small cairn that is the only sure key to the path. This is well cairned but rather indistinct in places, contours round the slopes below Bwlch y Moch, and then ascends over stony ground to a cairn perched on the northern spur of Crib Goch, above Dinas Mot. The cwm is now revealed on L. and is enclosed by mural precipices in which the Parson's Nose, a prominent cliff beloved by rock climbers, is centrally situated. The path skirts the western flanks of the spur and then continues along a grassy shelf, to end where the stream falls from Llyn Glas. A short step uphill brings it into view, and on its far side a level green stretch makes a good camping ground for climbers. This is a remote and delightful spot in which to soliloquise on a warm sunny day; for the rocky shelf holding the lake in its grip cuts off all sound of traffic in Llanberis Pass below, and the only sign of life is the occasional climber wending his way across the lofty ridge of Crib Goch on the southern wall of the cwm.

There are two exits that join Route 1: the first and easiest is to walk up beside the stream feeding the tarn in the direction of the Pinnacles, and then to climb the scree on R. to Bwlch Coch; the second is to go R. of the Parson's Nose, pass a tiny pool cupped in bare rock, and then to ascend the steep scree that emerges on the skyline near the summit of Crib y Ddysgl. In both cases Route 1 is followed to the summit of Snowdon.

5—TWP * *

Plate 59. ROUTE 10 BEGINS AT THIS POINT ON ROUTES 1 AND 2

Key Cairn

Pyg Track

Derelict Sheep Fold

Northern Spur of Crib Goch

Dinas Mot

Plate 60. ROUTE 10

Criby Ddysgl

Cwm Glas

Plate 61. First View of Cwm Glas from Route 10

Plate 62. Route 10—First Exit

Crib Goch

Pinnacles

Bwlch Coch

Camping Site

Llyn Glas

Clogwyn y Person (The Parson's Nose)

Llyn Glas

Plate 63. ROUTE 10—SECOND EXIT

THE GLYDERS GROUP

Glyder Fawr	. . .	3,279 feet
Glyder Fach	. . .	3,262 feet
Y Garn	. . . .	3,104 feet
Elidir Fawr	. . .	3,029 feet
Tryfan	. . . .	3,010 feet
Foel Goch	. . .	2,726 feet
Carnedd y Filiast	. .	2,694 feet
Mynydd Perfedd	. .	2,664 feet
Nameless Peak	. . .	2,636 feet
Bwlch Caseg-fraith	. .	2,588 feet
Elidir Fach	. . .	2,564 feet
Esgair Felen	. . .	2,500 feet
Gallt yr Ogof	. . .	2,499 feet
Bwlch Tryfan	. . .	2,350 feet

MAP 2
GLYDERS GROUP

WHEN seen from the south and west, the range of hills dominated by Glyder Fawr looks comparatively uninteresting as it merely displays a succession of vast grassy slopes interspersed here and there with outcropping rocks that are crowned by the sharp little top of the Castle of the Winds. The only notable exception is that of the single spur of Esgair Felen, whose reddish broken cliffs catch the eye and overhang the craggy declivities confined to this one point on this side of the group, bordered by the Llanberis Pass.

But when seen from the north this aspect changes dramatically and comes as a complete surprise; for one savage cwm follows another from east to west, all of them hemmed in by striking mural precipices. The range is further enhanced by the beautiful isolated peak of Tryfan, and amid the whole stands Ogwen Cottage, the hub of the many ascents from this side of the group.

Moreover, the summit ridge of the Glyders is unique in Wales and characterised by a grand display of chaotically arranged boulders whose desolate aspect vies with that of the main ridge of the Coolins, in the Misty Isle of Skye, for pride of place in wild Britain.

In view of these remarkable features it is not to be wondered at that the range draws legions of climbers, and there are so many routes up and over the group that many days can be spent in their exploration. All the important ascents are dealt with in the following pages, any or all of which may be climbed by persons in fit and vigorous condition. In snow, even on a clear day, climbing in the Glyders requires the utmost care when Alpine experience is a decided advantage.

GLYDER FAWR

Route 11. Ogwen Cottage and the Devil's Kitchen. Leave the Cottage by the rock staircase behind the new building

Plate 64. The enlarged Ogwen Cottage—Starting point of Routes 11-15, and 25-26, also 33

and ascend the stony track, which is often damp in places, and bear R. for Llyn Idwal. Pass the gate which opens up a revealing view of the first section of the route ahead, with the great cleft of the Devil's Kitchen on the skyline. Keep the lake R., pass Idwal Slabs L., and ascend the well-marked path which bears R. and eventually threads the immense boulders below the Kitchen. The retrospect from the mouth of the cavern is magnificent, with Llyn Idwal below, Llyn Ogwen in the middle distance and the Carneddau in the background, dominated by the shattered front of Pen yr Ole Wen. Now turn L. and climb the steep, boulder-strewn shelf to the skyline where a prominent cairn marks the route. Continue ahead past Llyn-y-Cwn R. and mount the twisting scree path which ultimately emerges on the broad summit of Glyder Fawr. This is one of the most desolate spots in Snowdonia, and a peculiarly shaped eminence of slate dominates this rocky top of the highest peak of the group.

The panorama from this stony wilderness is extensive, but restricted by the plateau-like top of the mountain. The view to the east along its wide ridge may first catch the eye, since its forlorn aspect suggests what might well be the surface of the moon. The Castle of the Winds appears below the great heap of stones that characterise Glyder Fach, about a mile distant, on L. of which rises the summit of Tryfan. To the south Snowdon and Crib Goch present a serrated skyline, and to the west Mynydd Mawr tops the ridge enclosing the Llanberis Pass, while to the north the vast bulk of the Carneddau stretches away in the distance, crowned by the prominent summits of Carnedds Ddafydd and Llywelyn. This coign of vantage stands at the head of four valleys, but to see them on a clear day involves a stroll round the rim of the plateau. They are: Nant Ffrancon to the Menai Straits; the Conway Valley to the sea near the Great Orme; Nant Gwynant to Harlech and the sea; and Llanberis Pass to Caernarvon.

Plate 65.   ROUTE 11—IDWAL SLABS

Devil's Kitchen

Idwal Slabs

Llyn Idwal

Plate 66. ROUTE 11

Glyder Fawr

Llyn y Cwn

Devil's Kitchen

Plate 67. LAST STRETCH OF ROUTE 11

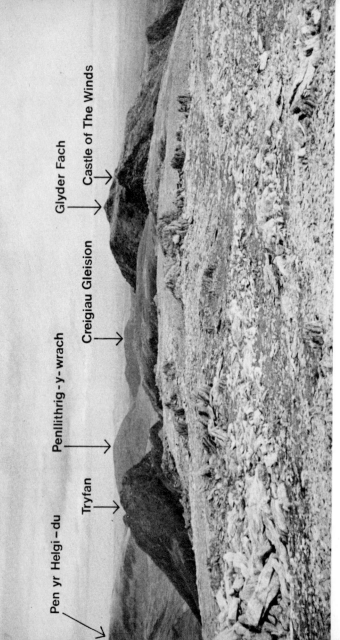

Pen yr Helgi-du

Tryfan

Penllithrig-y-wrach

Creigiau Gleision

Glyder Fach

Castle of The Winds

Plate 68. EASTERN PROSPECT FROM GLYDER FAWR

Nameless Cwm

Idwal Slabs

Llyn Idwal

Plate 69. Route 12

When this Route is used for the descent to Ogwen, it is worth while to pick up the stream from Llyn-y-Cwn and to follow it to the Devil's Kitchen, see plate 102, whence the path may be regained by crossing the grassy hummocks.

GLYDER FAWR

Route 12. Cwm Idwal and the Nameless Cwm. Follow Route 11 to Idwal Slabs, but bear L. up the grassy slopes before reaching them. When the Nameless Cwm opens up R., ascend the ridge above Idwal Slabs to the skyline, whence turn R. and walk up to the cairns on Glyder Fawr.

GLYDER FAWR

Route 13. The Gribin. Leave Ogwen Cottage by Route 11, and after passing the marshy section where the stones bear R., go straight ahead and climb the grassy slopes of the Gribin. A more interesting approach is to follow Route 11 almost as far as Idwal Slabs and to then climb L. up the steep grassy slopes which terminate on the lower section of the ridge. This variation has the element of surprise, in that on attaining the crest of the Gribin, Tryfan and Llyn Bochlwyd are suddenly revealed to the east, where the blue of the lake, surrounded by its green carpet of grass, contrasts strongly with the pale stony declivities of the mountain. The ridge rises gently at first over grass, with glimpses R. of the Devil's Kitchen and Y Garn, and eventually changes abruptly to rock. Climb carefully until its top is attained and then stride confidently ahead towards the disintegrated slabs of the Castle of the Winds, which fall L. precipitously into the cwm. Turn R. on the ridge, pass the forlorn hollow of the Nameless Cwm R., and follow the path through the stones and strange collections of crags to the summit of Glyder Fawr.

Bwlch Tryfan   Bristly Ridge   Glyder Fach   Castle of The Winds   Y Gribin   Nameless Cwm

Plate 70. ROUTE 13

Plate 71. Routes 14 and 15—seen from The Gribin

Bwlch Tryfan

Tryfan

Llyn Bochlwyd

Y Gribin →

Y Garn → Elidir Fawr → Carnedd y Filiast →

Plate 72. ROUTE 13—SEEN FROM TRYFAN

← Castle of The Winds

← Glyder Fach

Bristly Ridge →

Plate 73.   Route 13—Top of the Gribin

←——Tryfan

Llyn Bochlwyd——→

Plate 74. ROUTES 14 AND 15

GLYDER FAWR

Route 14. Llyn Bochlwyd, Bristly Ridge and Glyder Fach.
Follow Route 11 until the track bears R. and then go straight ahead by the line of cairns to the stream coming down from Llyn Bochlwyd. Climb beside it until this sombre lake comes into view and rest awhile by its shore to contemplate its wild situation. It is enclosed L. by Tryfan and R. by the Gribin, while ahead rise the cliffs supporting Glyder Fach which are a favourite playground for the rock climber. Proceed by keeping the lake R. and tread the gradually rising path which bears L. and eventually reaches the skyline of Bwlch Tryfan, enclosed L. by this wedge-shaped mountain and R. by Bristly Ridge. Pass the stone wall and turn R. where the route to the ridge is plainly visible since it bears the nailmarks of thousands of climbers who have passed this way. On reaching the base of the crags the track rises steeply and twists in and out of buttress and pinnacle, clearly marked throughout and quite safe for those with a steady head, to emerge finally on the broad stony ridge. Now turn R. and go over to inspect the Cantilever L., a great slab poised securely on vertical crags, whose top may be reached by an easy scramble. Then continue ahead to Glyder Fach L. whose massive pile of boulders is a conspicuous landmark hereabouts. Scramble to the top if you feel like it, but be careful, and then go over to the Castle of the Winds, with L. a fine prospect of Snowdon and R. a view of the gradually rising plateau ending at Glyder Fawr. It is better to climb straight over the Castle rather than take the circuitous course L. round its base, and descend carefully through the maze of vertical slabs of slate on its far side. Walk down to the col and there join Route 13 for the summit of the reigning peak of the group.

Plate 75. ROUTE 14—LLYN BOCHLWYD

Plate 76. RETROSPECT FROM ROUTE 14

Garnedd Llywelyn

Tryfan

Pen yr Helgi–du

Bristly Ridge

Plate 77. ROUTE 14—THE CANTILEVER

Plate 78. ROUTE 14—GLYDER FACH

Crib Goch

Snowdon

Crib y Ddysgl

Glyder Fawr

Castell y Gwynt

Plate 79. ROUTE 14

Route 15. Ogwen Cottage and Tryfan Scree Gully. Follow Route 14 to the stream but do not ascend the path beside it. Continue L. and pick up the track which rises steeply R., first over grass and finally by a conspicuous scree gully that emerges on the summit of Tryfan. This arduous route is not recommended.

Route 16. The North Ridge of Tryfan. This is one of the most interesting and entertaining scrambles in all Wales and the usual starting point is near the head of Llyn Ogwen, but the lower shoulder of the mountain may also be reached by a direct ascent from the other side of the ridge. Go through a gate L. of the Milestone Buttress and climb the long twisting staircase that first mounts beside a wall R. and later in the shadow of the Buttress itself. The track emerges on the shoulder which is covered with deep heather and has a cairn marking the meeting of several paths; it might even be called the Piccadilly Circus of Tryfan for tracks radiate and rise sharply up the North Ridge, the alternative approach from the east comes in, and it is the point of departure for Heather Terrace which rises diagonally across the eastern flanks of the peak at the foot of its three prominent buttresses. This landmark may be avoided by climbers who do not object to the ascent of a long scree slope, for one goes up from the bend in the track below this cairn. Thence there are so many variations in the route to the next shoulder that it is a matter of personal taste as to which of them is chosen, but that centrally situated can be most easily followed. Many parts of it are steep and slippery, and there are a few tricky bits where a conveniently placed handhold assists the passage. It rises diagonally R.

Cairn

To Milestone Buttress

To Milestone Buttress

Plate 80. START OF ROUTE 16

Bwlch Tryfan

Tryfan

Plate 81. ROUTE 16—SEEN FROM PEN YR OLE WEN

Elidir Fawr→   ↓Foel Goch   Mynydd Perfedd→

Llyn Ogwen

Plate 82. View R. of Route 16

round speculative corners and past the "Cannon", a huge leaning rock that is well seen from Ogwen, until eventually the second shoulder is attained. This platform calls for a halt, if only to scan the horizon which has widened enormously as height was gained. At this stage perhaps the most striking prospect is that of Llyn Ogwen, now far below, which even on sunny days looks black and forbidding against its brightly coloured engirdling hill slopes.

Ahead rises the last obstacle in this sporting course and since it consists entirely of rock it is best to tackle it direct from the point where the track ends against the cliff. However, there is an alternative L., where a faint path leads into the North Gully which is jammed with boulders and slabs to afford an enclosed variation to the other more exposed route. Both of them emerge on the North Peak, and it is only a short step to Adam and Eve, the two conspicuous upturned bolders that crown the summit of Tryfan.

On a sunny day it is usual to find a number of climbers gathered round this lofty perch; for it is a pleasant spot on which to eat lunch, to tackle the spectacular and risky "step" from Adam to Eve, and to enjoy the spacious panorama. The vista R. and L. along the valley extending from Capel Curig to Bethesda is of course attractive and divided by Llyn Ogwen far below. It is bounded on the north by the vast green slopes of the Carneddau whose broad ridges culminate in Carnedd Llywelyn. But their smooth flanks do not attract the eye so strongly as the immediate landscape of the Glyders themselves, where Llyn Idwal and Llyn Bochlwyd sparkle on the floor of the rockbound cwms stretching westwards. Bristly Ridge forms a broken wedge to the south, and the eye wanders R. over the ridge to the crags supporting the Gribin, passing centrally the very tip of Snowdon which will be missed even on a clear day by those who do not possess an alert and discerning eye! Farther R. the skyline rises gently to Glyder Fawr, and then after a fall to the Devil's Kitchen rises again

Plate 83.   ROUTE 16—ADAM AND EVE

to Y Garn and continues westwards in an almost flat line to Foel Goch, above which the curving ridge of Elidir Fawr will draw the eye. Thence it passes over Mynydd Perfedd, finally to merge with the rising slopes of Pen yr Ole Wen.

There is still a long way to go to Glyder Fawr and in consequence the climber must not linger too long on his airy seat; so begin the descent by crossing the crest that leads to the South Peak and glance back at the summit of Tryfan to grasp more clearly its isolated situation. Then carefully descend the twisting track which passes in and out of gaps between the boulders and eventually reaches a little col separating the main peak from its shapely satellite, on top of which L. lies a charming rock-bound pool reflecting the colour of the sky. Now bear R. and wander down the clearly marked path to Bwlch Tryfan, there to join Route 14 to the crowning peak of the group.

Y Garn   Elidir Fawr   Foel Goch

Plate 84. ROUTE 16—WEST FROM TRYFAN

GLYDER FAWR

Route 17. Heather Terrace. If you come by car, park it at the farmhouse of Wern-y-gof-uchaf, which stands back from the road L. just above the head of Llyn Ogwen, and clearly reveals Heather Terrace as a diagonal line rising across the face of Tryfan. Leave the back of the farm and pass L. some inclined slabs which are used as a practice ground by rock climbers. Then join the path R. which crosses some marshy ground and later rises over scree to the cairn noted in Route 16. Now proceed in and out of a collection of boulders that stand amid thick heather and bilberries to gain the Terrace, which follow upwards past the base of the three buttresses and their adjacent gullies, all of which rise into the sky right up to the summit of Tryfan and afford one of the most treasured playgrounds of the rock climber. Bear R. at the termination of the Terrace and go over a low stone wall to the col, at which point join Route 16 for the remainder of the ascent.

Plate 85.   ROUTE 17—SEEN FROM HELYG

GLYDER FAWR

Route 18. Bwlch Caseg-fraith. The ridge rising to this pass from the Ogwen Valley is one of the most revealing and least used in this group of hills. It is a paradise for the photographer, and as long ago as 1941 I gave an account of it in my *Snowdonia through the Lens*, when a friend came with me from Helyg to Pen y Pass over the Glyders in superb Alpine conditions. Yet, although I have since ascended it on several occasions I have never encountered another climber or photographer with whom I could share the rare beauty of the magnificent scenes it unfolds.

The key to this route is the farmhouse of Gwern-y-gof-isaf, which nestles at the very root of the ridge on the south side of the Afon Llugwy, almost opposite Helyg, and is reached by crossing a picturesque bridge from the main highway. Those who come by car may park the vehicle near the farm. The ridge rises in grassy steps, interspersed with crags which become more plentiful as height is gained; it is enclosed R. by Cwm Tryfan and L. by Nant yr Ogof. About half-way along its crest there is a grand prospect of Tryfan across the cwm, and from this height the peak assumes its true elevation and under snow assumes the splendour of an Alpine giant. The ridge steepens and later flattens out on a lofty plateau rimmed with crags, on which repose Llyn Caseg-fraith and two smaller pools. They are priceless gems in a sombre setting, and on a calm day reflect the upper buttresses of Tryfan to perfection. There is also a splendid view of Bristly Ridge L., whose pinnacles and buttresses are clearly delineated by the sunlight before noon. A rather indistinct track threads the soft marshy ground hereabouts, and on leaving the platform it swings R. and crosses the Miners' Track coming up from Pen-y-gwryd and going over to Bwlch Tryfan beneath the crags of Bristly Ridge. Thereafter it skirts the rim of Cwm Tryfan and eventually joins Route 14 at the top of Bristly Ridge.

Plate 86. ROUTE 18—BUTTRESSES OF TRYFAN

Bristly Ridge

Tryfan

Plate 87. STARTING POINT OF ROUTE 18

Plate 88.　Tryfan from Route 18—Bwlch Caseg-fraith.

Miners' Track to Ogwen →

Plate 89. BRISTLY RIDGE SEEN FROM ROUTE 18

Plate 90. LLYN CASEG-FRAITH—RETROSPECT FROM ROUTE 18

GLYDER FAWR

Route 19. Gallt yr Ogof. This rounded craggy eminence is the first of the Glyder group to come into view L. when proceeding westwards along the Holyhead road from Capel Curig. It may be reached conveniently from the road by crossing the Afon Llugwy, whence a nice scramble up a conspicuous diagonal gully places the climber on the skyline. Here you turn L. for the summit and then bear R. for the Nameless Peak whose far side slopes down to Llyn Caseg-fraith. Here you join Route 18 for Glyder Fawr.

GLYDER FAWR

Route 20. The Ridge from Capel Curig. The long and lofty ridge of this group begins almost at the very doors of the village and its complete traverse, followed by the descent from Glyder Fawr to Ogwen Cottage, requires good weather and a long day. The best approach to it is by the lane L. of the post office. Cross the bridge with the noisy cataract R. and follow the old Ogwen road to the last cottage, then bear L. over grass and rock until the higher ground is attained. If a direct line along its crest is taken several craggy eminences will be encountered, and it may be desirable to turn them on L. or R. In due course pass round the rim of Nant y Gors R. and make for the Nameless Peak to join Route 19 for the remainder of the long tramp.

Plate 91. ROUTE 19—GALLT YR OGOF FROM THE HOLYHEAD ROAD

Cave

Plate 92. ROUTE 19

← Gallt yr Ogof

Plate 93. ROUTE 20

GLYDER FAWR

Route 21. Pen-y-gwryd and the Miners' Track. This popular path begins at a stile below the hotel and at a bend in the road opposite Llyn Lockwood. It takes a more or less direct line for the end of a stone wall running uphill R., which is reached after crossing the stream coming down over bare slabs from Llyn Cwmffynnon. The ground hereabouts is very boggy and even when climbing beside the wall several very wet patches are encountered. These terminate on passing through a gap in a cross wall, near a sharp corner L. Thence a cairned track slants uphill R. through rock and heather, and at the end of this steep section it is worthwhile to look back at the fine vista down the Vale of Gwynant, and R. to the Snowdon Horseshoe. Now continue the ascent at an easier gradient, past a waterfall L. until a break in the rock ridge overhead gives access to vast areas of marshy ground on the summit plateau. Go forward until Llyn Caseg-fraith appears ahead. Here join Route 18 to Glyder Fawr L., or if proceeding to Ogwen Cottage follow the well-marked track that contours round the head of Cwm Tryfan, below the crags of Bristly Ridge.

Plate 94. VALE OF GWYNANT FROM ROUTE 21

Plate 95. ROUTES 21 AND 22—THE GLYDERS FROM PEN-Y-GWRYD

Pen y Gwryd ←

Plate 96. STARTING POINT OF ROUTE 21

GLYDER FAWR

Route 22. Pen-y-gwryd and Llyn Cwmffynnon. This is the most direct route from the south to the reigning peak of the group. Go through the yard behind the hotel and follow a runnel uphill for a time, then bear L. and cross the peaty ground to the outflow of the lake. Continue R. round its shore and on reaching the stream entering it from the Glyders walk by its banks and take the L. branch which rises through the wide opening of Heather Gully. The going is very rough but not as steep as it looks from afar, and the route terminates quite suddenly by the cairns on Glyder Fawr. If the main stream is followed it will lead to the col below the Castle of the Winds, but by bearing L. on reaching the grassy slopes and later R. the summit of Glyder Fawr may be attained.

GLYDER FAWR

Route 23. Pen y Pass and Esgair Felen. Cross the road from the car park and ascend the new track which starts immediately to the east of the last building. It rises gently through the crags on the R. and on reaching the skyline it opens up a comprehensive view of Llyn Cwmffynnon and the Glyders. Turn L. up the long grassy shoulder of Glyder Fawr, past a remarkably perched boulder L., and when near the top of the slope bear L. for the conspicuous red precipitous crags of Esgair Felen. This is a magnificent coign of vantage for the appraisal of the Crib Goch–Crib y Ddysgl section of the Horseshoe, for the view into Cwm Glas opposite with the stream falling steeply to the pass below, and for the long vista down the Llanberis Pass to the twin lakes at Llanberis. Then turn round and ascend the broad ridge that terminates on the summit of Glyder Fawr.

Glyder Fawr

Castell y Gwynt

Llyn Cwmffynnon

Plate 97. ROUTE 22

Plate 98. LLANBERIS PASS FROM ESGAIR FELEN

Esgair Felen

Glyder Fawr

Dinas y Gromlech

Plate 99. TERMINAL STRETCHES OF ROUTE 23

ELIDIR FAWR

This peak is one of the more westerly of the Glyders group, and presents a fine wedge-shaped elevation when seen from the Carneddau (see plate 135). If climbed from Ogwen by way of Y Garn the distance to be covered is almost 10 miles and involves an ascent of about 3,500 feet. Whereas if approached from Deiniolen, on the west, the distance is reduced to less than 6 miles with about 2,000 feet of ascent as the starting point is already 1,200 feet above sea level.

Route 24. To reach Deiniolen cross the bridge at the foot of Llyn Padarn and later turn R. At the end of the village a narrow walled lane leads L. to the new quarries, where, with permission, you may park your car near the building inside the main gate. Return to it for the grassy cart track that goes off to the L. and follow it until you come to a stile on the R. This gives access to a wide stretch of marshy ground where the muddy track leads to a grassy spur, surmounted by a wall beside which it continues to Marchlyn Bach, and thence to Marchlyn Mawr, a larger sheet of water hemmed in on the R. by a ring of crags. This wall is continuously straight and a good guide in misty weather. Follow the narrow track on the L. of Marchylyn Bach and in due course climb some 400 feet of grassy slopes to the broad ridge above Marchlyn Mawr which tops the 2,000 feet contour. You will observe a sketchy track running below the crags and eventually rising to the dip in the skyline. This is Bwlch y Brecan, on the L. of which the ridge rises to Mynydd Perfedd. Now turn R. and ascend the rim of the cwm above the crags, in which the squarish Pillar of Elidir is prominent. On reaching the top, join the path coming in on the L. from Ogwen and turn R. to follow it to the Cairn on Elidir Fawr. This lofty coign of vantage opens up a wide panorama round the western arc, and includes Anglesey and unusual prospects of the Snowdon range.

Marchlyn Mawr

Marchlyn Bach →

Plate 100. ROUTE 24 FROM MARCHLYN BACH

Bwlch y Brecan

Pillar of Elidir

Plate 101. ROUTE 24 FROM MARCHLYN MAWR

Carneddau

Llyn Ogwen

Llyn Idwal

Plate 102. LOOKING DOWN THE DEVIL'S KITCHEN

Route 25. Ogwen Cottage and Llyn Clyd. These two mountains make a picturesque backdrop to the western prospect from the head of Llyn Ogwen, and when seen by morning light a dark shadow is cast into the wild cwm immediately below the summit of Y Garn, in which repose, out of sight from this viewpoint, the small tarn of Llyn Clyd and a placid pool just above it. The direct ascent of this peak is tough and unyielding, and there are two well-defined tracks: the fishermens route is if anything less steep and rises L. of the stream to end at Llyn Clyd; the climbers' route is some distance R. and takes a direct line for the grassy ridge hemming in the cwm.

Follow Route 11 to Llyn Idwal and bear R. along its shore. Pass round a boggy hollow and then ascend one or other of the alternative tracks already mentioned. Keep to the well-trodden path which rises along the crest of the ridge all the way to the cairn on Y Garn, and meanwhile note the wild prospect of the cwm below L. The isolated summit of Y Garn is a grand viewpoint and to the south unfolds a grim prospect of Snowdon and its satellites, with R. views of Llanberis and the sea on a clear day. But it is the Glyders themselves that will hold the gaze, for their rocky cwms are disclosed to perfection across the void. Tryfan and Llyn Ogwen will catch the eye to the east and the riven declivities of Pen yr Ole Wen on the other side of Nant Ffrancon to the north contrast strangely with the smooth green slopes of the Carneddau in the background. Now walk in a north-westerly direction and keep to the rim of the cwm R. all the way to Foel Goch, whose cairn is scarcely as revealing as that of Y Garn. This tramp, together with the return descent, is enough for the average pedestrian's day, but strong walkers should continue along the lofty ridge to Mynydd Perfedd which opens up a striking prospect of Elidir Fawr L.. with Marchlyn Mawr R. Those bound for Llanberis

Plate 103. Route 25—Y Garn from Llyn Ogwen—Alternative Starts

Llyn Clyd

Plate 104. ROUTE 25—WILD CWM ON Y GARN

Carneddau

Tryfan

Llyn Ogwen

Llyn Idwal

Plate 105. **RETROSPECT FROM ROUTE 25**

Plate 106. ROUTE 25—SNOWDON FROM Y GARN

Lliwedd — Crib Goch — Snowdon — Carnedd Ugain — Clogwyn Du'r Arddu

Esgair Felen — Cwm Glas

Bristly Ridge   Glyder Fach   Castle of The Winds   Nameless Cwm   Glyder Fawr

Y Gribin

Llyn y cwn

Plate 107.   Route 25—The Glyders from Y Garn

←Elidir Fawr

Carnedd y Filiast →

Mynydd Perfedd →

Foel Goch →

Plate 108. ROUTE 25—SEEN FROM Y GARN

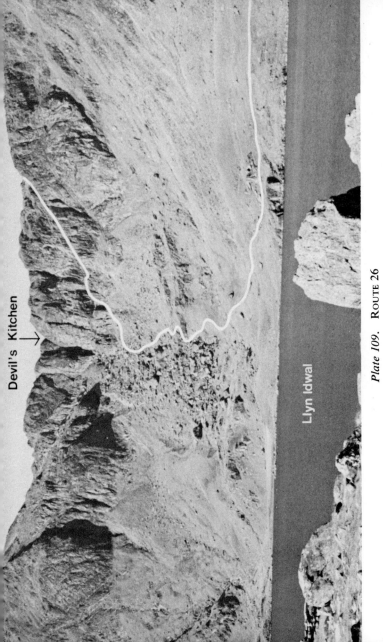

Devil's Kitchen →

Llyn Idwal

Plate 109. ROUTE 26

may traverse this peak and descend round the slate quarries to Llyn Peris or follow Route 24 down to Deiniolen.

Y GARN

Route 26. Ogwen Cottage and the Devil's Kitchen. Follow Route 25 to the boggy hollow and pick up the track L. that skirts Llyn Idwal with splendid views of Idwal Slabs L. Then continue its ascent through the boulders to the Kitchen, and bear R. to climb the shelf which emerges at the foot of the grassy slopes of Y Garn. Keep Cwm Idwal R. and on encountering craggy ground glance down to Llyn Clyd before attaining the cairn on the summit of this peak.

Plate 110.   Idwal Slabs from Route 26

THE CARNEDDAU

CARNEDD LLYWELYN	3,484 feet
CARNEDD DDAFYDD	3,426 feet
PEN YR OLE WEN	3,210 feet
FOEL GRACH	3,195 feet
CRAIG LLUGWY	3,184 feet
YR ELEN	3,151 feet
FOEL FRAS	3,091 feet
YR ARYG	2,875 feet
LLWYTMOR	2,749 feet
PEN YR HELGI-DU	2,732 feet
PENLLITHRIG-Y-WRACH	2,621 feet
DRUM	2,528 feet
CRAIG EIGIAU	2,389 feet
CREIGIAU GLEISION	2,213 feet
PEN Y CASTELL	2,034 feet
TAL-Y-FAN	2,000 feet
CLOGWYN MAWR	1,500 feet

THE Carneddau comprise the largest group of hills in Snowdonia and consist mainly cf broad grassy ridges, scantily interspersed with outcrops of rocks, save the well-known cliffs of Craig yr Ysfa, Black Ladders and the steep shattered southern front of Pen yr Ole Wen.

They afford excellent walking country, free from major problems, but the distances to be covered in their exploration are misleading to the eye, and, moreover, the vast plateau-like summit of Carnedd Llywelyn is one of the mistiest spots in the group.

The enormous whale-back ridges, though in places well cairned, can be difficult in mist owing to the absence of well-defined landmarks, and in bad weather walks should be confined to the ascent of one or other of the peaks within easy reach of the Ogwen Valley. To make a successful traverse of the range in these conditions requires expert use of map and compass, together with long experience of the group as a whole, but on clear days no difficulties should be encountered.

The following routes include most of the popular ascents, but in view of the vast distances from the well-known centres of the most northerly tops they have been omitted from this work.

MAP 3
CARNEDDAU—SOUTH

THE CARNEDDAU

Route 27. Llyn Crafnant and Clogwyn Mawr. The easy walk to this lovely lake through a charming wild valley is one of the delights enjoyed by every visitor who stays in Capel Curig, and if desired may include Llyn Geirionnydd on the return journey. However, the former may also be reached by car from Trefriw and the latter by driving sharp L. at the Ugly House. Hence, by combining walking with riding this enchanting corner of the Carneddau can be seen with the minimum of effort.

The route for pedestrians leaves Capel by the gate opposite the post office. Follow the path past the conspicuous Pinnacles R., then cross a stream where the ground is often damp, and go through another gate into some woods at the foot of a rocky eminence L. On emerging from the trees walk over the flat stones laid throughout in damp places, then cross another stream and continue uphill at an easy gradient until the valley comes into view ahead. Now pass round a vast stretch of marshy ground L. and later bear R. into the upper reaches of the valley which is hemmed in L. by the craggy ridge that culminates in Clogwyn Mawr. Continue ahead through rock and heather until the watershed is reached, whence pass through a wall and stroll downhill to the sylvan shore of Llyn Crafnant.

Clogwyn Mawr appears on the skyline L. from the highest point of the path. Bear L. here by a less distinct track and on reaching higher ground keep R. until a cairn is encountered in thick heather. Then zigzag more steeply through the scattered crags, taking whichever way is fancied, and eventually bear L. to attain the little plateau whose summit cairn is conspicuous at its western end. The vista along the Ogwen Valley suddenly bursts upon the eye and will doubtless come as a great surprise. Looking round the great arc from L. to R. the panorama reveals:

Llyn Crafnant →

Plate 111. CAPEL CURIG POST OFFICE—ROUTES 27 AND 28 START HERE

Plate 112. ROUTES 27 AND 28—THE PATH TO LLYN CRAFNANT

Clogwyn Mawr
→

Llyn Crafnant

Path

Plate 113. Route 27—Lake and Path from Slopes of Clogwyn Mawr

Moel Siabod and the Llynnau Mymbyr, Moel Hebog and part of the Snowdon Group, the immense mass of the Glyders, Tryfan, Foel Goch and the Carneddau from Pen yr Ole Wen to Creigiau Gleision. There is also a bird's-eye view of Llyn Crafnant.

THE CARNEDDAU

Route 28. Creigiau Gleision. This lofty ridge is nearly three miles due north of Capel Curig and the most easterly peak in the Carneddau, over 2,000 feet in height. It is supported by a long line of broken crags, its crest is over a mile in length, and on the west its slopes fall steeply to Llyn Cowlyd. On the east, however, its gradient is easier but dappled with crags, beneath which plantations of conifers descend to the shore of Llyn Crafnant.

Follow Route 27 to Clogwyn Mawr, pass the cairn and descend steep grass on its north side. Cross a wall at its highest point and pick up the track beyond it which leads to a large sheepfold immediately at the foot of Craig Wen, a prominent rocky eminence conspicuous in the view from Clogwyn Mawr. Continue along the now less distinct track, keeping all craggy outcrops well R. and on skirting the last of them the summit of Creigiau Gleision comes into view R. The cairn stands on the highest section of the long ridge and opens up extensive views to the east, in which the blue of several tarns and lakes will catch the eye. To the west, however, views of the Carneddau are restricted by Penllithrig-y-wrach on the other side of Llyn Cowlyd, but the south-western arc discloses Moel Siabod, the Glyders, Tryfan and Y Garn to advantage. Creigiau Gleision may also be reached by diverging R. when Llyn Cowlyd comes into view during the ascent of Route 29.

Snowdon   Glyders   Gallt yr Ogof   Tryfan   Mynydd Perfedd

Plate 114. ROUTE 27—VISTA OF THE OGWEN VALLEY FROM CLOGWYN MAWR

Plate 115. RETROSPECT OF ROUTE 28

Creigiau Gleision

Plate 116. LAST STRETCH OF ROUTE 28

Plate 117. ROUTE 28—THE SUMMIT OF CREIGIAU GLEISON

Plate 118. Route 29—The View from Tal-y-waun

Route 29. Penllithrig-y-wrach. This pointed peak is the last sentinel on the ridge descending to the south-east from the dominating peak of the group, and is a conspicuous object when seen from Capel Curig. Walk along the Holyhead road from the village and after passing Bronheulog go through a narrow gate R. and follow the track past Tal-y-waun L. The direction is clearly indicated by some power lines which are in single file at first and double on the higher ground ahead. The terrain hereabouts is notoriously wet and boggy, and it is better to bear L. and pick up a line of white-tipped posts which later veer R. to join the more direct route. A leat is eventually encountered, and although the more athletic climber may spring across it and land on a muddy bank, it is advisable to turn L. until a bridge appears ahead. Walk over a plank just short of it and bear R. over a stile, whence the path opens up a fine prospect of Llyn Cowlyd below, enclosed by Penllithrig L. and by Creigiau Gleision R. Now cross another plank L. over a stream and make for a clearly marked grassy depression that terminates on the skyline, crossing several rocky outcrops *en route*. Then bear R. over steep grass until the cairn surmounting Penllithrig appears on the skyline. The vast panorama round the south-western arc is revealing and includes all the familiar peaks from Moel Siabod to Carnedd Llywelyn, with below the latter a good view of Craig yr Ysfa R. of the grassy Pen yr Helgi-du.

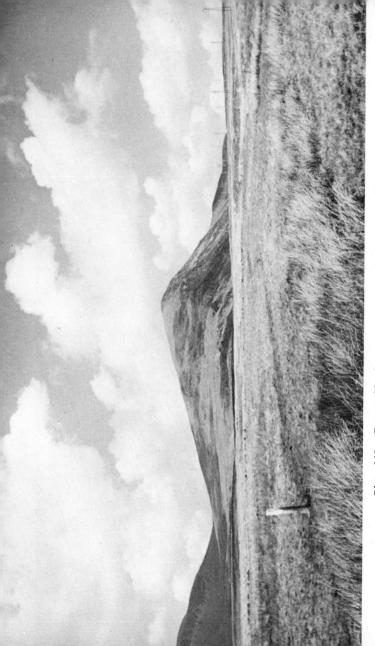

Plate 119. ROUTE 29—PENLLITHRIG-Y-WRACH FROM THE MOOR

Plate 120.   THE VIEW OF LLYN COWLYD FROM ROUTE 29

Plate 121. ROUTE 19—LAST STRETCH TO THE SUMMIT

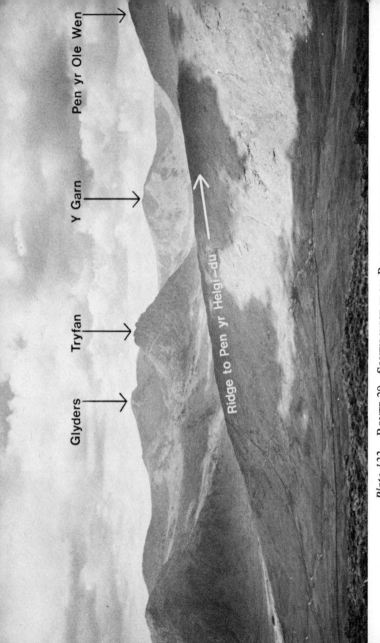

Pen yr Ole Wen

Y Garn

Tryfan

Glyders

Ridge to Pen yr Helgi—du

Plate 122.   Route 29—South-west from Penllithrig-y-wrach

Carnedd Ddafydd   Pen yr Helgi – du   Craig yr Ysfa   Carnedd Llywelyn

Plate 123.   Route 29—West from Penllithrig

Route 30. Pen yr Helgi-du. This is the culminating point of the grassy ridge that takes root at Tal-y-braich, and its cairn is about two miles north of the Holyhead road. It may be conveniently approached from Helyg, and the indistinct track rises through heather and bracken to a leat bringing water down from the Afon Llugwy L. to Llyn Cowlyd R. Cross the wooden bridge, pass a sheepfold and bear R. to attain the lower slopes of the broad ridge, then keep to its gradually ascending crest until the cairn is reached. The fall to the north is steep and rocky, and those wishing to extend their walk may do so by crossing the narrow ridge to Craig yr Ysfa L., or by tramping over the broader ridge to Pen llithrig-y-wrach R. The spacious views unveiled from the summit are interesting and reveal the blue of Llyn Eigiau to the north, the hills about Capel Curig to the east, Gallt yr Ogof and the wedge of Tryfan to the south, and the precipitous crags of Craig yr Ysfa, crowned by the immense summit of Carnedd Llywelyn, to the north-west. By moving over to the edge of the summit plateau L., a bird's-eye view is obtained of Ffynnon Llugwy, which occupies the floor of the wild cwm below. Pedestrians ascending this ridge *en route* for Carnedd Llywelyn may avoid the last rise to its summit by following a track L. which provides an almost level course to the connecting ridge.

THE CARNEDDAU

Route 31. Helyg, Craig yr Ysfa and Carnedd Llywelyn. This walk is one of the most interesting and revealing ascents in the Carneddau, and if the descent is made by reversing one or other of the following two routes it yields the finest circuit in this lofty group of hills, and, moreover, is the most rewarding to the photographer.

Leave the road to the west of Helyg and follow the path which keeps straight ahead, with Pen yr Helgi-du R. Pick

Pen yr Helgi-du   Penllithrig-y-wrach

Plate 124. ROUTE 30

Plate 125. ROUTE 30—CRAIG YR YSFA FROM PEN YR HELGI-DU

Pen yr Ole Wen →

Plate 126. ROUTE 31—HELYG—THE CLIMBERS' CLUB HUT

up a disused mining road that comes up from the moor L. and go through a gate leading up to a derelict building, from which point the retrospect is worthy of note with Bristly Ridge and Tryfan L. and Y Garn above Llyn Ogwen R. Continue L. along the grassy mine track with Pen-y-Waen-wen ahead, and on reaching Ffynnon Llugwy below L. climb the twisting path that emerges on the ridge R. of this eminence. Here a carpet of heather and bilberries makes a luscious foreground to the spacious view of Cwm Eigiau, with the blue of the lake shimmering in the distant north-east and L. a prospect of the sharply falling crags of Craig yr Ysfa. Turn L. along the ridge and scramble to the top of these cliffs by a well-worn track, but before attaining the summit glance back at the route so far ascended with Ffynnon Llugwy below. Halt awhile on the rim of Craig yr Ysfa which discloses the vast Amphitheatre, hemmed in on either side by sheer cliffs that are the treasured playground of the rock climber. Note also the undulating ridge R. which displays the sharp drops on the northern flanks of both Pen Llithrig-y-wrach and Pen yr Helgi-du. Then continue the walk by ascending the long ridge that terminates on the summit of the reigning peak of the group.

The top of Carnedd Llewelyn is a vast, almost square plateau, and is a place to be avoided in mist owing to the difficulty in locating the safe ways off the peak. It supports a large cairn and its mossy surface is dappled with stones and strangely contorted groups of boulders. The panorama on a clear day is best seen by strolling round the rim of the plateau, and while it splendidly reveals the broad grassy ridges of this group trailing away to the north, with the shapely peak of Yr Elen L., it is the south-western arc that will hold the gaze. The Glyders, Snowdon and the top of Pen yr Oleu-wen lead the eye R. to the long ridge of Carnedd Dafydd, with R. a glimpse of the distant Rivals, Moel Elio and the beautiful sharp cone of Elidir Fawr, with still further R. the sea stretching to infinity.

Plate 127. RETROSPECT FROM ROUTE 31

←—Craig yr Ysfa

Ffynnon Llugwy

Plate 128. ROUTE 31

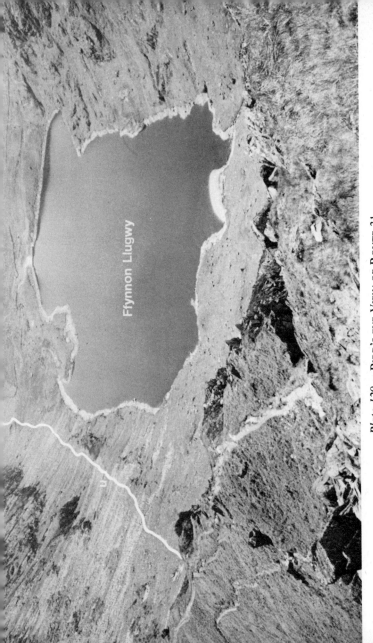

Frynnon Llugwy

Plate 129. BIRD'S-EYE VIEW OF ROUTE 31

Cwm Eigiau

Plate 130.   ROUTE 31—PRECIPICES OF CRAIG YR YSFA

Plate 131. CRAIG YR YSFA FROM CWM EIGIAU

Pen yr Helgi–du

Penllithrig–y–wrach

Cwm Eigiau

Plate 132. THE LAST ASCENT OF ROUTE 31

Plate 133. Route 31—Summit Cairn on Carnedd Llywelyn

Yr Elen →

Plate 134. ROUTE 31—VIEW FROM SUMMIT

Plate 135. ROUTE 31—SUNSET FROM CARNEDD LLYWELYN

Route 32. Llyn Ogwen and Carnedd Ddafydd. Pass round the head of Llyn Ogwen and walk up to the farmhouse of Tal-y-llyn Ogwen, above which follow the Afon Lloer into the wide mouth of the wild cwm above. Turn L. and make your way through the crags at the foot of the eastern spur of Pen yr Ole Wen, and above them ascend over grass until the track L. from this peak is encountered. Glance down into the cwm R. and note the rough triangular shape of its lake, then follow the well-worn stony track R. whose ups and downs are clearly seen as far as the summit of Carnedd Ddafydd. Before proceeding look back at the view whose skyline reveals the Glyders, Crib Goch and Snowdon above the enclosing slopes of Ffynnon Lloer, with R. the tops of Y Garn, Craig Cwmsilyn and Mynydd Mawr. Then turn your steps in the direction of Carnedd Llywelyn, which now appears as an uninteresting but massive grassy hill. Descend L. over the stones to a cairn and look down on the grim bastions of Black Ladders R., whose almost vertical cliffs are seldom visited by the rock climber. Pass round their craggy rim by Craig Llugwy and make your way over the broad stony ridge to the summit of the highest peak of the group.

Pen yr Ole Wen

Ffynnon Lloer

Tal-y-llyn Ogwen

Llyn Ogwen

Plate 136. THE START OF ROUTE 32

Plate 137. CWM LLOER SEEN FROM ROUTE 32

Carnedd Ddafydd

Ffynnon Lloer

Plate 138. ROUTE 32

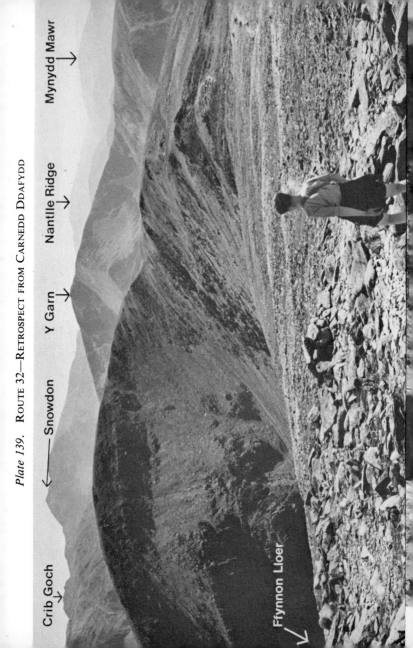

Plate 139. Route 32—Retrospect from Carnedd Ddafydd

Crib Goch · ──Snowdon · Y Garn · Nantlle Ridge · Mynydd Mawr

Ffynnon Lloer

Plate 140. BLACK LADDERS FROM ROUTE 32

Carnedd Llywelyn

Cwm Llafar

Plate 141. FINAL ASCENTS OF ROUTES 32 AND 34

Plate 142. ROUTE 33—PEN YR OLE WEN FROM OGWEN COTTAGE

THE CARNEDDAU

Route 33. Ogwen Cottage and Pen yr Ole Wen. The direct ascent of this lofty sentinel is by far the toughest in all Snowdonia and should only be undertaken by climbers who revel in the ascent of slippery scree that is almost everywhere overgrown with deep heather.

Leave the Cottage and walk over the bridge L. Scramble over the wall R. and then over the rocks to gain the steep grassy slopes ahead, whence a narrow path winds its way aloft. On reaching a rough platform the real collar work begins, and although the ascent may be continued by any of the indistinct tracks through the heather, it is easier to bear R. until the edge of the slope is reached and then zig-zag L. to the first top. Now climb over boulders to the second and real summit of the peak, beyond which walk along the grassy path to join Route 32 on the lip of Cwm Lloer.

The view to the south from Pen yr Ole Wen is one of the most striking in the region, because it not only discloses a remarkable prospect of the North Ridge of Tryfan, but also a superb vista right into Cwm Idwal far below. Glyder Fawr appears above Idwal Slabs, and Crib Goch, Snowdon and Crib y Ddysgl above the Devil's Kitchen. Climbers should note that photographs of these dramatic scenes are best taken in the late afternoon of a clear summer day, when the westering sun illuminates the deep cwm to perfection by the elimination of too much shadow.

Plate 143. Tryfan and Llyn Ogwen from Route 33

Plate 144. ROUTE 33—CWM IDWAL FROM THE SUMMIT

Gwaun-y-gwiail

Plate 145. STARTING POINT OF ROUTE 34

THE CARNEDDAU

Route 34. Bethesda and Carnedd Llywelyn. This ascent
begins with a long walk up a pleasant and spacious valley
and concludes with a stiff climb at its head. In consequence
the views are restricted until the peak is gained.

Leave the main street in the town at the police station and
follow the uphill road to the bus stop where it forks; the
right branch terminates at Gwaun-y-gwiail which stands at
the broad mouth of Cwm Llafar. Follow the path with the
Afon Llafar L. and cross its tributary, the Afon Cenllysg,
to continue beside the main stream. Ascend the path which
mounts between it and the slopes of the steep ridge surmounted with crags R. and with the grim cliffs of Black
Ladders ahead. When Nant Ddu and Nant Fach join the
Afon Llafar, follow the latter to its source beneath Carnedd
Llywelyn. Then climb the steep grass to the ridge R. of the
peak, whence bear L. for its immense summit. A longer
variation takes in Yr Elen, which is reached by walking for
about a mile along the path, whence bear L. up its western
slopes, and after passing its craggy summit keep to the
narrow ridge, with steep drops L. to the diminutive Ffynnon
Gaseg, until the crowning peak of the group is attained.

245

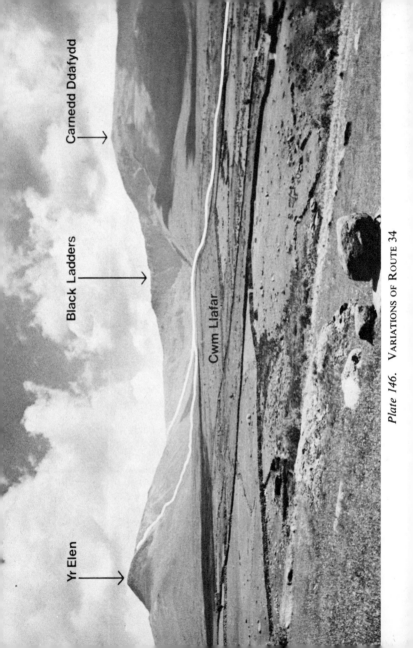

Yr Elen   Black Ladders   Carnedd Ddafydd

Cwm Llafar

Plate 146. VARIATIONS OF ROUTE 34

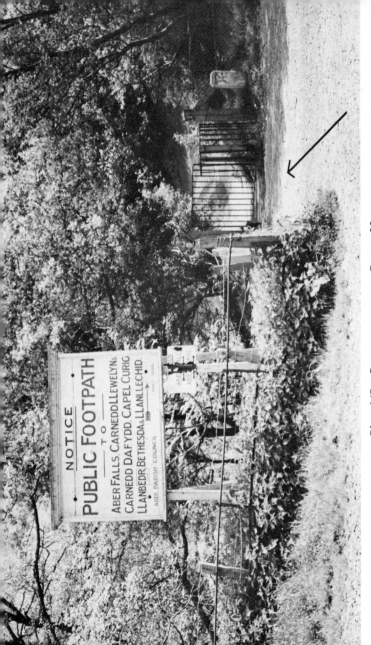

Plate 147. STARTING POINT OF ROUTE 35

MAP 4
CARNEDDAU—NORTH

THE CARNEDDAU

Route 35. Aber Falls and Carnedd Llywelyn. This long walk is sometimes undertaken by climbers staying as far away as Capel Curig, and the only convenient way of doing it is to persuade someone to drive you to Aber in the morning and to pick you up at an agreed spot in the Ogwen Valley in the late afternoon. The usual starting point is Pont Newydd, with two car parks, reached from Aber by a charmingly wooded side road.

The path goes through a gate R. of the bridge and is clearly marked as it winds its way beneath abundant trees for about two miles. It ends immediately opposite Aber Falls, where the Afon Goch takes a dramatic leap over some 200 feet of cliff: when the stream is in spate this splendid display should on no account be missed. The track to Carnedd Llywelyn bears L. about half a mile short of the fall and rises gradually across a vast scree slope. It then takes an exposed course on rocky slopes L., with sensational drops R. to the base of the fall, and thereafter mounts over grass beside the musical cascades of the stream R. After passing a prominent sheepfold the valley widens considerably, with the craggy top of Llwytmor L., and Bera Mawr R., crowned with immense crags, whence the stream is followed as far as its source between Foel Fras L. and Yr Aryg R. Now bear R. across a marshy track and climb the latter peak, whence follow the broad grassy ridge south over Foel Grach to Carnedd Llywelyn, with views R. of the craggy ridge of Yr Elen below which nestles the tiny tarn of Ffynnon Caseg. Strong walkers may vary this route by leaving the Afon Goch at the sheepfold and ascending over grass to the rocky summit of Bera Mawr, but unless you are a rock climber avoid its more precipitous crags. Thence keep to the rising contours west of Yr Aryg and after crossing the spur of Foel Grach circle round Cwm Caseg and scramble up to the lofty connecting ridge of Yr Elen, which visit before attaining Carnedd Llywelyn.

Plate 148. ROUTE 35—ABER FALLS

Plate 149.   ROUTE 35—THE STREAM BELOW THE FALLS

Bera Mawr

Plate 150. ROUTE 35—ABOVE THE FALLS

THE MOEL SIABOD GROUP

MOEL SIABOD	.	.	.	2,860 feet
MOELWYN MAWR	.	.	2,527 feet
MOELWYN BACH	.	.	.	2,334 feet
ALLT FAWR	.	.	.	2,287 feet
CNICHT	.	.	.	2,265 feet
YSGAFELL WEN	.	.	.	2,192 feet
MOEL DRUMAN	.	.	.	2,152 feet
MOEL YR HYDD	.	.	.	2,124 feet

THE shapely peak of Moel Siabod is the northern sentinel of a vast upland area, dappled with lakes and tarns, that sprawls in a south-westerly direction to end with the Moelwyns in the east and Cnicht in the west. It is perhaps strange that the topography of the group reveals so few mountains worthy of attention, and were it not for the graceful tapering lines of the latter which, when seen end-on from the south-west is reminiscent of the Matterhorn, it might well escape the notice of climbers. As it is, there are few who tread its isolated summit, and fewer still who scale and traverse the more distant Moelwyns. Nevertheless, there is no doubt that the group as a whole affords grand walking country, and especially that part of it centred round the attractive blue of Llyn Edno.

Since Moel Siabod overlooks Capel Curig, this is the obvious starting point for its shortest ascent, but it should be borne in mind that owing to the easy gradient of its grassy slopes it may be climbed from any side; that from the east, however, involves the crossing of much boggy ground and in consequence is the least popular approach.

Route 36. The Royal Bridge and Moel Siabod. Leave the village by the Royal Bridge, a wooden structure spanning the outflow of Llynnau Mymbyr, and note the splendid prospect of the Snowdon Group R. Then cross a stile giving access to the immense spruce plantations clothing the lower hillside and mount the path that winds its upward way through them, eventually to emerge from the leafy canopy with the foreshortened view of the peak on the skyline ahead. Now make your way to the top where a succession of large flat rocks deck the crest of the ridge, with sensational views L. down the cliffs to Llyn y Foel, and pave the way to the cairn standing amid a chaotic collection of boulders. A variation of this route goes L. above the trees and eventually reaches the crest of the north-eastern ridge of the mountain. It has the advantage of spacious views on either hand during the greater part of the ascent.

The panorama from Moel Siabod is of exceptional interest owing to its isolated position on the eastern fringe of Snowdonia, and while its extensive views round the south-western arc well disclose both near and distant objects, including Dolwyddelan Castle below, it is the western prospect of a galaxy of peaks and valleys that will rivet the gaze. The Snowdon Group first catches the eye and on the L. of Lliwedd appears the sharp cone of Yr Aran, with further L. Moel Hebog and its satellites. Below them there are glimpses of Llyn Dinas and Llyn Gwynant. To the R. of Snowdon rise the Glyders, with both Bristly Ridge and the top of Tryfan prominent above the intervening ridge, and with further R. the conspicuous sloping top of Pen yr Ole Wen leading the eye to the tremendous landscape of the Carneddau, where Carnedd Llywelyn appears above the falling craggy ridge of Gallt yr Ogof.

MAP 5
MOEL SIABOD GROUP—NORTH

Moel Siabod

Plate 151. ROUTE 36—MOEL SIABOD FROM THE ROYAL BRIDGE

Moel Siabod

Plate 152. VARIATIONS OF ROUTE 36

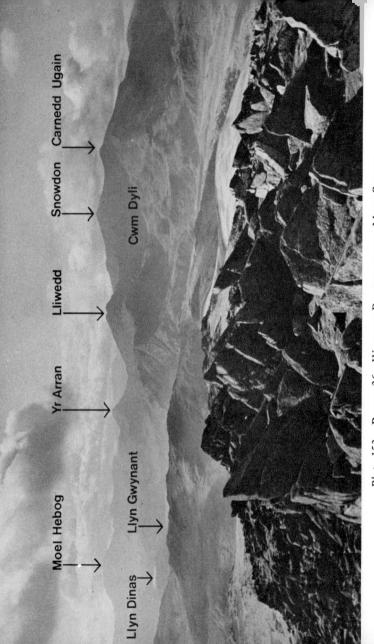

Moel Hebog Yr Arran Lliwedd Snowdon Carnedd Ugain

Llyn Dinas Llyn Gwynant Cwm Dyli

Plate 153. Route 36—Western Prospect from Moel Siabod

Plate 154. Route 37

THE MOEL SIABOD GROUP

Route 37. Cyfyng Falls, Llyn y Foel and Moel Siabod.
This is the finest and most rewarding ascent of the dominating peak of the group, because it unfolds a close view of its
precipitous eastern front, an aspect that is not clearly
revealed from more distant viewpoints.

Walk down the road from Capel Curig and turn R. over
the stone bridge spanning Cyfyng Falls. These are worthy
of notice when the Afon Llugwy is in spate and a good
viewpoint will be found farther down the highway. Avoid
the first fork R. over the bridge, but bear R. at the second
and ascend the old quarry road which; on emerging from
the trees, passes an attractive farmhouse R. Thereafter
continue along the now grassy road across the open moor,
with views R. of Capel Curig below and of the subsidiary
top of Moel Siabod straight ahead. In wet weather the
grassy road ends in very boggy ground, but it can be
avoided by taking the track on the R. which leads to a wire
fence. Cross it and turn sharp L. to pass round a rocky
spur and then rejoin the path. Now go ahead past a
sheet of water L. until the old slate quarry buildings are
reached, whence continue over a rise ahead when Llyn y
Foel comes into view, hemmed in R. by the rocky bastions
of the peak. Walk L. round the tarn and pass its outflow
to gain the foot of the broken ridge rising to its summit.
Climb along the edge of the crags for the view down into
the wild cwm R. and find a way in and out of the rocks and
boulders until the cairn appears suddenly on the skyline.
Climbers wishing to by-pass Llyn y Foel may go straight
ahead from the wire fence and ascend slippery grass
between rocky outcrops on either side. On attaining the
crest, bear R. for the ridge of your peak.

Plate 155. ROUTE 37—CYFYNG FALLS IN SPATE

Moel Siabod

Llyn y Foel

Plate 156. FINAL ASCENT OF ROUTE 37

Plate 157. CNICHT FROM TAN-LAN

MAP 6
MOEL SIABOD GROUP—SOUTH

THE MOEL SIABOD GROUP

Route 38. Cnicht by the Dog Lakes This is one of the most delightful walks in the whole group and allows plenty of time for browsing in the heather beside one or other of the lovely tarns that are passed on the way. A car is useful for getting to Nanmor, because it not only saves time which may be spent more pleasantly on the higher ground, but it also facilitates the descent of Cnicht by reversing Route 40 if the vehicle is driven round to Croesor.

Drive along the charming Vale of Gwynant and turn south for the sequestered valley of Nanmor by crossing the bridge that spans the Afon Glaslyn near Bryn y Dinas. Drive carefully up the steep and narrow side-road between stone walls, and if another vehicle is encountered one must enter a field R. near the top to allow the other to pass. At its highest point the road turns sharp R. near two gates and there is enough space here to park two cars. Go through the gate R. and descend across pasture to reach the Afon Llyn Edno, which follow uphill all the way to its source. The immediate ascent is the steepest and roughest section of the walk, and passes through a number of romantic little gorges on the slopes of Moel Meirch L. It is worth while to look back from time to time, since the scene discloses the twisting course of the lower section of the Watkin Path, dominated by Bwlch Main and Snowdon, with L. a view of Llyn Dinas and of Moel Hebog and some of its satellites.

This route is the only sure way to locate Llyn Edno, because it is cradled in a shallow basin dappled with crags, and from other directions may be difficult to find; it is said to be full of trout and the local fishermen's paradise. Halt here awhile to enjoy the fine view and note the excellent prospect of the Snowdon Horseshoe to the north-west, where Yr Wyddfa appears above Lliwedd and the ridge R. encompasses Crib y Ddysgl, the Pinnacles and Crib Goch. Before leaving this secluded and enchanting spot, walk round the south shore of the lake for the vista

Plate 158. Route 38 Follows the Course of Afon Llyn Edno

Llyn Edno

Moel Meirch

Space for 2 Cars

Snowdon Crib y Ddysgl Crib Goch

Llyn Edno

Plate 159. ROUTE 38

Plate 160. ROUTE 38—SUMMIT RIDGE OF CNICHT

Yr Aran →   ← Snowdon   Crib Goch →   Glyders →

Cwm y Llan

← Llyn Dinas

Plate 161. ROUTE 38—PANORAMA FROM CNICHT

Moel Hebog   Craig Cwmsilyn   Nantlle Ridge   Y Garn II   Mynydd Mawr

Plate 162.   ROUTE 38—PANORAMA FROM CNICHT

Glyders   Penllithrig-y-wrach   Moel Siabod   Summit Ridge of Cnicht

Plate 163.   ROUTE 38—PANORAMA FROM CNICHT

across it of Moel Siabod whose graceful lines are especially pleasing to the eye. Extensive marshes lie to the east, and are the source of the Afon Lledr, which, after passing Dolwyddelan with its famous castle, flows into the River Conway in the vicinity of Betws-y-coed.

Now ascend the nearby curving ridge of Ysgafell Wen which encloses these marshes, and walk south along its crest to the Dog Lakes, a collection of tiny tarns of which Llynnau Cwn R. is the largest. It also unfolds another excellent view of the Horseshoe, in which, however, the precipitous eastern front of Yr Wyddfa is now clearly disclosed. Then go ahead past Llyn yr Adar R., and above Llyn y Biswail also R., to reach the base of the long summit ridge culminating in Cnicht. There are a few ups and downs on its crest and the cairn stands at its far end, overlooking Tremadoc Bay. But by following this route to the peak its most surprising and striking feature is revealed in the sudden precipitous drop into Cwm Croesor, which gives the impression of perhaps 3,000 feet whereas in fact it is only about 1,700 feet. Beyond rise the Moelwyns, whose graceful sweep is marred by unsightly and now disused quarry workings. The panorama round the southern arc is extensive, with Tremadoc Bay seemingly almost at one's feet, the Harlech Dome L. backed by the distant cliffs of Cadair Idris, and the Arans and Arennigs still farther L. But it is the vast panorama of Snowdonia that will hold the gaze, for this lofty and isolated peak is so placed that it reveals a chain of mountains that stretch right round the north-western arc: it is perhaps the finest coign of vantage in the whole region. The Moel Hebog group L. comprises the reigning peak, the Nantlle Ridge and Mynydd Mawr; the centrally situated Snowdon group assumes graceful lines with views right into Cwm-llan where the Watkin Path is clearly seen in a limpid atmosphere; the skyline R. comprises the Glyders, Penllithrig-y-wrach in the Carneddau, and ends with the nearer graceful peak of Moel Siabod.

Note.—Walkers who wish to avoid the tricky scrambling through the lower gorges of the Afon Llyn Edno should pass through the gate and follow the road on the R. to the farm of Hafodydd Brithion. Beyond it they could pick up a sketchy track that ultimately joins Route 38 near a sheepfold in more open country.

THE MOEL SIABOD GROUP
Route 39. Cnicht by Llyn Llagi. This is a shorter variation of Route 38 and to reach its starting point it is necessary to drive farther along the Nanmor road and to park the car at the slate quarry where there is room for several vehicles. At the former chapel, now Blaen Nant, the track comes up from the foot of Llyn Dinas by way of the farm of Hafod Owen and continues on the other side of the road.

Follow it down to the farmhouse and pass to the L. behind it to gain the rocky track rising to a gate beside the cascading stream. Continue ahead by a path through heather and bracken, with the murmuring stream R., and follow it all the way to its source in Llyn Llagi. Cross several walls *en route*, of which only one has to be climbed over, and when the gradient eases off walk by the wall R. across grass to the lake. This remarkable circular sheet of water has a sombre and wild setting, and steep crags enclose its far side, broken in one place only by a perfectly straight gully that carries down the outflow from Llyn yr Adar, 600 feet above. Now continue the walk by skirting the shore L. and make for the straight gully already mentioned. Experienced climbers may like to tackle it direct L., but those who prefer an easier though more circuitous ascent may follow a cairned track up the valley on the L. which later turns R. and contours up the hillside to the skyline. On reaching Llyn yr Adar, pass round it and join Route 38 for Cnicht.

272

Plate 164. Converted Chapel in Nanmor—Starting point of Route 39

Llyn yr Adar

Llyn Llagi

Plate 165. Route 39—Seen from the Chapel

Llyn yr Adar

Llyn Llagi

Plate 166. HARDEST SECTION OF ROUTE 39

Cnicht →

Plate 167. FARM AT CROESOR—ROUTE 40 BEGINS HERE

Route 40. Cnicht from Croesor. This ascent is just a hard grind and it begins at Croesor. This tiny secluded hamlet is encircled by Green hills and reached by a narrow side-road from Garreg, a village on the eastern flanks of the Glaslyn Valley. Access to the side road is gained by a sharp turn under the attractive lodge of Plas Brondanw.

Begin the ascent by turning R. below the chapel and walk up the side road to a farm. Go through a gate R., pick up an indistinct track and at the fork take the L. branch. This rises diagonally across the hillside, with Cnicht towering overhead, crosses several walls and on reaching a green hollow continues ahead until the crest of the rough ridge is attained. Keep to the ups and downs of the grassy track which takes a direct line for the peak. The last section is steep and there are two alternative routes: that L. is the more popular because it includes some easy scrambling over rock and scree; that R. is easier, grassy and less sensational, but joins the other just below the cairn. The record for the ascent and descent is held by Mr. Showell Styles, who accomplished it in winter in 1 hour 18 minutes!

Plate 168. ROUTE 40—RIDGE RISING TO CNICHT

Plate 169. FINAL ASCENT OF CNICHT BY ROUTE 40

Moelwyn Mawr   Craig Ysgafn   Moelwyn Bach

Plate 170.   ROUTE 41—THE MOELWYNS FROM THE AFON GLASLYN

THE MOEL SIABOD GROUP

Route 41. The Moelwyns from Croesor. These hills comprise three tops fairly close together and they make a fine skyline when seen from the Afon Glaslyn on the west side of the valley. Unhappily, the northern slopes of Moelwyn Mawr are spoilt by unsightly and now disused quarry workings, and of the many possible routes to the peak this ascent is chosen because it does not disclose them until the summit cairn is attained.

Leave transport in the square at Croesor and return to the cross roads at the entrance to the hamlet. Go straight ahead, or if coming from Garreg turn sharp R., and walk as far as the first gate on the resurfaced single-track road going over the low hills to Tal-y-bwlch. Then turn L. and ascend the grassy slopes beside a stone wall, and on reaching the top of this rise the Moelwyns come into view ahead. Now bear L. and cross a wall surmounted by a wire fence, and then go straight on over grass by a very indistinct track to the ridge L. that rises to Moelwyn Mawr. It is clearly marked by a wire fence that runs up to a conspicuous stone tower, probably used long ago in connection with the quarry R. of the peak. Finally climb the steep shaly slopes above and follow the craggy rim of the cwm L. to attain the cairn at the far end of the ridge.

On a clear day the panorama round the north-western arc is of the first order and not unlike that already described from Cnicht, save that this mountain is in a direct line with Snowdon and therefore obscures the lower reaches of Cwm-llan. However, it has a unique feature in that immediately to the north the blue of some twelve tarns is disclosed in the sunlight and there is also a striking view of Moel yr Hydd R. Moreover, there is a more spacious prospect of the sea beyond Portmadoc and the southern arc reveals the Arennigs, the more distant Berwyns, the great mass of the Harlech Dome, backed by the cliffs of Cadair Idris.

Plate 171. CROESOR FROM ROUTE 41

Moel Hebog ←

Nantlle Ridge →

Now descend the grassy slopes to Craig Ysgafn, whose craggy summit is well seen from Moelwyn Mawr. Keep L. over this very rough top and note the conversion of Llyn Stwlan into a reservoir far below, with Blaenau Ffestiniog beyond. Descend the steep terminal crags of this eminence L., with steep drops also L., and follow the nail marks down to the col. Then go ahead and climb Moelwyn Bach by grass and crags L., or by easy grass slopes R., and walk over to the last cairn which opens up a superb prospect of all the peaks in Mid-Wales. The easiest way off this peak is to keep to the broad grassy ridge descending west all the way to the resurfaced road and so back to Croesor. Do not attempt to shorten the route by descending R. into the vast hollow, as it is dappled with bog and extensive stretches of marshy ground, beyond which several walls and fences have to be crossed to reach the road.

Moelwyn Mawr →

Plate 172. ROUTE 41

Moel Hebog →

Nantlle Ridge →

Mynydd Mawr →

Cnicht

Plate 173. Summit Ridge of Moelwyn Mawr and Route 40 from Route 41

Moelwyn Bach

Craig Ysgafn

Moelwyn Mawr

Plate 174. ROUTE 41 OVER THE MOELWYNS

THE MOEL HEBOG GROUP

MOEL HEBOG . . .	2,566 feet
CRAIG CWMSILIN . .	2,408 feet
TRUM Y DDYSGL . . .	2,329 feet
GARNEDD GOCH . . .	2,301 feet
MYNYDD MAWR . . .	2,290 feet
CLOGWYN MARCHNAD .	2,286 feet
MYNYDD TALMIGNEDD .	2,148 feet
MOEL LEFN . . .	2,094 feet
MOEL YR OGOF . . .	2,020 feet

MOEL HEBOG completely dominates the charming village of Beddgelert, which occupies the floor of the valley at the three cross-roads, and effectively shelters it from the prevailing south-westerly winds. Its elevation is foreshortened from this near viewpoint, but its shapely stature is seen to greater advantage from the bridge over the Afon Glaslyn half a mile north of the village, and better still from the more distant head of Llyn Dinas when it is framed between the hills enclosing the lower stretches of the Vale of Gwynant. Its finest elevation, however, is revealed from Pont Cae'r-gors which spans the Afon Colwyn some two miles north on the road to Caernarvon, when its graceful tapering lines are especially attractive by late afternoon light. The ascent of this mountain makes a pleasant and easy afternoon walk, but if its immediate satellites, Moel yr Ogof and Moel Lefn, are included, then a full day is necessary for the average pedestrian.

Moel Hebog

Cwm–Cloch.

Plate 175. Starting point of Route 42

MAP 7
MOEL HEBOG GROUP

THE MOEL HEBOG GROUP

Route 42. Beddgelert and Moel Hebog. The key to this route is the farmhouse of Cwm-cloch, which may be reached by a fingerposted path through the fields behind the Royal Goat Hotel, or by going a short distance up the Caernarvon road and turning L. over the Afon Colwyn. This bridge gives access to a by-road that passes under the long-disused Welsh Highland Railway and thence through a small pine wood to the farm. Go through a gate beside a farm building opposite and cross the usually wet pasture by a line of flat stones to a break in its far wall, beyond which a well-cairned path rises through heather and bracken. A large cairn, built on an immense boulder, will be observed high up the slope ahead and this is the key to the turning point in the route. It stands on a broad ridge in sight of the plantations and like many others on this mountain is flecked with white quartzite. It is worth while to pause here, if only to scan the scene round the northern arc, because, strange as it may seem, many of the engirdling hills look more imposing from this viewpoint than they do from the higher summit cairn. Although the Snowdon group should hold the gaze, it does not do so owing to its less interesting southern aspect, and in consequence the eye wanders R. to skim along the lovely stretches of the Vale of Gwynant in which the blue of Llyn Dinas contrasts beautifully, and especially so in autumn, with its enclosing hills, to rest finally upon the lovely outline of Moel Siabod. Farther R. Cnicht and the Moelwyns stretch across the skyline above the sylvan approach to the Aberglaslyn Pass, when the sharper elevation of Moelwyn Mawr from this angle will catch the eye. Now turn L. at this key cairn and climb the ridge to a gate in a wall, whence a line of cairns lead uphill to the L. corner of the precipitous front of the peak. Then bear R. and scramble up its rocky edge to the summit.

Moel Hebog

Cwm–Cloch

Plate 176. UPPER SECTION OF ROUTE 42

The cairn on Moel Hebog stands some distance back from its precipitous front and thus opens up the south-western prospect of Cardigan Bay to advantage. The engirdling hills slope down gently to its shore and disclose among other eminences a fine outline of the Rivals away to the west. But to observe the northern arc it is advisable to descend slightly as Beddgelert is then disclosed over 2,000 feet below, backed by the Snowdon group and the Vale of Gwynant, a grand scene indeed.

Climbers wishing to extend this walk may do so by descending to the north along the edge of the ridge leading to Moel yr Ogof and continue over grass for a further mile to Moel Lefn. This top opens up a spacious prospect of the Pennant Valley L. and of the Nantlle Ridge to its R. Continue the descent to the pass below and follow the path above the plantations to Rhyd-ddu, or bear R. through them for a shorter return to Beddgelert.

An exhilarating ridge walk, known as the Pennant Horseshoe, combines the traverse of the two satellites of Moel Hebog with a section of Route 43. It starts in Cwm Pennant at Pont-y-plas, where there is room to park one car near the bridge, rises to Moel yr Ogof and follows the ridge to Moel Lefn. Thence there is a considerable loss in height before reaching a wall ladder which gives easy access to the ascent of Trum y Ddysgl. On attaining the cairn Route 43 is followed to Garnedd Goch, whence the descent to Pont-y-plas is made by Cwm Ciprwth.

Moel Hebog →

Plate 177. Final Ascent of Route 42

Plate 178. BEDDGELERT FROM ROUTE 42

Moel Siabod

Llyn Dinas

Plate 179. VIEW FROM ROUTE 42

THE MOEL HEBOG GROUP

Route 43. The Nantlle Ridge. The walk in either direction over the hills forming this interesting and revealing ridge, which encloses Drws-y-coed Pass on the south, is doubtless the finest in this group and competes favourably with some of the better-known ones in Snowdonia. Its remote situation on the western fringe of the region makes it a prize for the connoisseur, and although I have traversed its crest from each end on several occasions I have only twice encountered other climbers on this route.

Since transport to either end of the ridge is desirable, and, moreover, as it is possible to walk there and back along its crest in a long day, it is a question of deciding at which end to begin and where to leave the vehicle, unless, of course, it can be driven from the starting point to meet the climber who only makes the one-way traverse in the day. Those who are interested in photography will find the light favourable for an east-west traverse in the morning and also for the return in the afternoon, but others who wish to engage in rock climbing on the great slab in Cwm Silyn would do better to leave their transport at that end. Furthermore, not only is it easier to attain the ridge by first climbing Craig Cwmsilyn, but this course avoids the longer circuitous climb to the cairn on Y Garn II. If the latter ascent is chosen, then the car may be parked in a wide section of the road below Bwlch Gylfin, on the 700 feet contour about a mile west of Rhyd-ddu. But if the former, then it should be driven past Llyn Nantlle Uchaf, along the first fork L. to the hamlet of Tan yr Allt, and then sharp L. up a narrow twisting mountain road that ends in a field beyond a farm L. on the 880 feet contour, where it may be parked within easy reach of Cwm Silyn.

On the assumption that the climber carries a camera, I shall describe the Nantlle Ridge from east to west, but it

Plate 180. SNOWDON FROM THE SLABS OF Y GARN II

Y Garn II

Craig-y-Bere

Mynydd Mawr

Llyn y Gadair

Plate 181. ROUTE 43—FIRST SECTION

Mynydd Drws—y—coed

Y Garn II

To Bwlch Gylfin

PATH
To Carddnant mill
FOLLOW ARROWS

Plate 182. ROUTE 43—FINAL SECTION

should be understood that some of my studies illustrating this route were in fact taken on the return walk. The two variations of the ascent of Y Garn II described in the first edition are not yet freely accessible, although those who wish to climb the peak by its north ridge, past the vertical slabs shown in Plate 180, may possibly obtain permission from the local farmer.

Alternatively, the mountain could be climbed by first walking along the little-used path to Pennant. This leaves the road at a gate on the L. about half a mile from Rhyd-ddu, at the first sharp bend to Bwlch Gylfin. Follow the wall to a farm gate, whence bear L. uphill and follow the arrows in the direction of the distant plantations. But do not leave this track until you pass through another gate, from which point bear R. for a conspicuous stream in a shallow gully. Ascend its R. bank and later diverge L. to easier ground. On attaining the broad grassy ridge bear R. and walk up to the stony summit and cairn on Y Garn II.

The extensive panorama from this lofty sentinel is justly magnificent and reveals the whole of the western aspect of the Snowdon group to perfection, with the cottages of Rhyd-ddu far below and R. the cone of Yr Aran above the shimmering blue of Llyn y Gadair. To the north there is a fine view of the shattered crags of Craig y Bere on the other side of the pass, and below the rounded summit of Mynydd Mawr. To the west the first two tops surmounting the ridge are well seen and there are glimpses of the others R., with farther R. Llyn Nantlle Uchaf and the sea, while to the south the broad ridge culminates in Moel Hebog.

Now turn your steps westwards and pick up the grassy track beside a stone wall L., pass the exit of a deep gully R., and start the rocky climb to the summit of Mynydd Drws-y-coed. Be careful near the top when turning L. to step across a gap where rock projects above, and then keep to the edge of the summit cliffs with a big drop R. On the other side descend through crags and beyond the col

Rhyd-ddu

Plate 183.   ROUTE 43.   SNOWDON FROM Y GARN II

Plate 184.   ROUTE 43—CRAIG Y BERE FROM Y GARN II

Mynydd Drws-y-coed

Plate 185. THE TRICKIEST SECTION OF ROUTE 43

Mynydd Talmignedd

Craig Cwmsilyn

Trum y Ddysgl

Plate 186. Ridges of Route 43, seen from Y Garn II

Craig Cwmsilyn   The Rivals   Mynydd Talmignedd

Plate 187.   HIATUS ON ROUTE 43

follow the grassy path to the summit of Trum y Ddysgl which opens up a good backward view of the ridge and of the immense cairn on Mynydd Talmignedd. Continue down a long grass slope and make for the connecting ridge below, which has eroded so badly that the path descends L. to pass this hiatus at the saddle. Then walk up to a short length of wall and go L. of it to reach the conspicuous obelisk on this summit. It is so large that it can be seen from a great distance on a clear day and is said to have been built by quarrymen whose hobby was the erection of this pillar. The summit of Mynydd Talmignedd opens up a fine prospect of Craig Cwm Silyn, with the narrow rock ridge rising to its cairn from Bwlch Drosbern, a little-used pass from Nantlle to Pennant. The distant Rivals can be seen R. above the cwm, with a glimpse of one of the tarns below, and this viewpoint is one of the few from which the castles of Caernarvon, Cricieth and Harlech can be seen simultaneously. Continue the traverse by walking downhill towards the next peak on the ridge, and beyond the pass exercise care while climbing the rock ridge ahead, with steep drops L., until the cairn on Craig Cwm Silyn is attained. Rest here awhile to admire the superb retrospect which unfolds the whole of the undulating ridge, backed by Snowdon. Then continue westwards and bear R. over a wilderness of rocks until Cwm Silyn appears below R. and note the tremendous slab which is the venue of expert rock climbers, and beneath which are cradled the two glittering tarns. Descend the rim of the cwm and make for the locked gate, beyond which a grassy cart road leads direct to the car park. This is the usual terminus of the traverse, but those who wish to continue to Garnedd Goch from Craig Cwm Silyn may walk over a mile of almost level stony ground, past two large cairns, whence grass and a wall lead to the final cairn on the ridge.

Plate 188. LOOKING BACK TO HIATUS ON ROUTE 43—FROM THE OBELISK

The Rivals →

Cwmsilyn

Craig Cwmsilyn

Plate 189. LAST ASCENT ON ROUTE 43

Plate 190. Route 43—Retrospect of the Ridge from Craig Cwmsilyn

Garnedd Goch

Cwm Silyn

Plate 191. Route 43—Optional Extension and Final Descent

Plate 192. THE GREAT SLAB IN CWM SILYN—SEEN FROM ROUTE 43

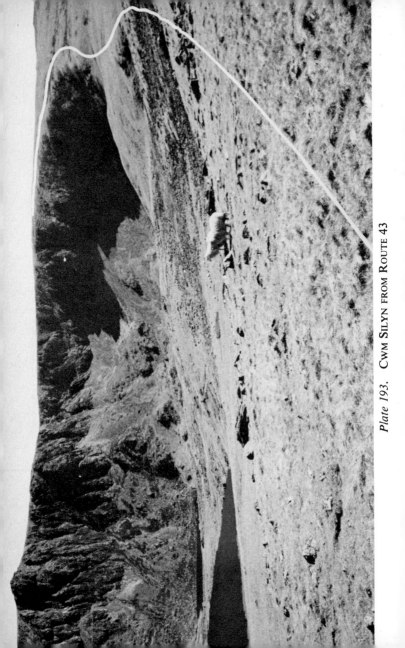

Plate 193. CWM SILYN FROM ROUTE 43

THE MOEL HEBOG GROUP

Route 44. Craig y Bere and Mynydd Mawr. Both Y Garn II and Craig y Bere are clearly visible from the road near Llyn y Gadair, and the shattered crags of the latter overhang the northern slopes of Drws-y-coed Pass. To attain them and then continue to the summit of Mynydd Mawr is an afternoon excursion which can be started conveniently from Planwyd Farm, situated on the L. of the highway near the head of Llyn Cwellyn. Thence a road threads the Plantation, which the Forestry Commission permit the public to use as far as the second gate, near a building on the R. Here a grassy break in the trees on the L. carries the power lines over the crest of the hill. Follow this grassy path, and on reaching open ground overlooking the Nantlle Valley turn R. by the wire fence and continue along the well-marked path, crossing the stiles provided. Then ascend the steep grass of Foel Rudd which forms the prominent shoulder of your peak, and from which the retrospect of Snowdon and Llyn Cwellyn below is worth noting. Thereafter keep to the path which passes to the R. of Craig y Bere as shown in Plate 196. Here you may rest awhile to observe the scene of chaos at your feet and of the ups and downs of the Nantlle Ridge on the other side of the pass, now far below. Then follow the track which rises at an easy gradient over stony ground until the cairn on Mynydd Mawr appears on the skyline. The extensive flat summit discloses Anglesey and the sea to the north, but limits the appraisal of the vast panorama of hill and valley in other directions. Snowdon is, of course, supreme, and L. appear Glyder Fawr with a glimpse of Tryfan over its shoulder, then Y Garn encloses the higher tops of the Carneddau between them, while R. of Snowdon the skyline encompasses both Cnicht and the Moelwyns.

Craig y Bere

Plate 194. Starting point of Route 44

Craig y Bere

Mynydd Mawr

Llyn y Dywarchen

Plate 195. UPPER SECTION OF ROUTE 44

Craig y Bere

Mynydd Mawr →

Plate 196. Route 44 passes to the R. of Craig y Bere

Llyn y Dywarchen →

← Llyn y Gadair

Plate 197. ROUTE 44—THE PRECIPICES OF CRAIG Y BERE

Plate 198.   ROUTE 44—PROSPECT OF SNOWDON FROM CRAIG Y BERE

Plate 199. The Nantlle Ridge from Route 44

Plate 200. MYNYDD MAWR FROM THE NORTH

CADAIR IDRIS

PEN Y GADAIR	. . .	2,927 feet
MYNYDD MOEL	. . .	2,804 feet
CRAIG Y CAU	. . .	2,500 feet
GAU GRAIG	. . .	2,400 feet
TYRAU MAWR	. . .	2,200 feet
CRAIG LAS	. . .	2,167 feet
CRAIG LLYN	. . .	2,040 feet
BWLCH RHIWGWREFYDD	.	1,838 feet
LLYN Y GADAIR	. . .	1,837 feet
LLYN Y CAU	. . .	1,552 feet
LLYN Y GAFR	. . .	1,400 feet

MAP 8
CADAIR IDRIS

CADAIR IDRIS is one of the three chief mountains of Wales and ranks second only to Snowdon in popularity. Its summit is 2,927 feet above sea level, and although forty-three feet lower than Aran Fawddwy, the highest peak in Mid-Wales, it completely dominates the district. Consisting of alternate strata of Felspathic trap and shale, it takes the form of a high ridge and extends for some eight miles between Cross Foxes on the east and Arthog on the west. Its northern front is precipitous and girt with crags which are broken in one or two places only; that of the scree slope carrying the Foxes' Path is the most noteworthy. Beneath the crags are ranges of foothills, and below these again lie the Mawddach Estuary and the town of Dolgellau. Several rugged spurs extend southwards from the ridge and give easy access to Tal-y-llyn and the Dysynni Valley, but one of them bends eastwards to form a grand rocky cwm in the bosom of which rests the stygian waters of Llyn y Cau. This magnificent scene is frowned upon by the steep, riven crags of Craig y Cau, the whole forming one of the wildest places in all Wales.

Cadair Idris is the traditional "Chair" of Idris, a giant whom the old bardic writings represent as having been at once poet, astronomer and philosopher, and who, moreover, is alleged to have studied the stars from his rocky seat on the summit of this peak. The chair is the gigantic hollow immediately to the north of Pen y Gadair and is hemmed in on the east by the Foxes' Path, and on the west by the narrow, shattered ridge of Cyfrwy. It cradles the lonely waters of Llyn y Gadair.

The extraordinary popularity of the mountain is due in part to its accessibility and ease of ascent from all points, but more especially to the extensive panorama unfolded to the north from the entire length of its crest. This superiority of outlook is accounted for by its position in relation to the Mawddach Estuary and the valleys extending thence to Traws-fynydd Lake in the north and Bala Lake in the north-east.

Plate 201. CADAIR IDRIS FROM THE NORTH

Route 45. Tal-y-llyn, Cwm y Cau and Pen y Gadair.
There are at least eight routes of ascent, three from each
side of the ridge and one from each end of it, but the finest
of them all is that from Tal-y-llyn. Walk beside this
sequestered lake and continue ahead along the road to the
gates of the Idris property, a distance of about two miles.
Pass through the gates and enter an avenue of conifers L.,
which in spring is embellished by colourful rhododendron
blossoms. Cross a bridge and then a stile, and turn R. to
ascend the path that rises steeply through trees beside the
stream coming down from Llyn y Cau. Pass the precipitous, rocky bluff of Ystradgwyn that is shagged with
conifers R., and on emerging from the leafy canopy leave the
usual path that rises through bracken L., cross the stream
and then ascend its L. bank to walk westwards below the
long line of cliffs. There is no track and this detour involves
perhaps a mile, but it has the advantage of revealing a
complete frontal view of Cwm y Cau. The broken cliffs
of the immense crag, together with the detached obelisk
of the Pencoed Pillar L., rise above a boulder-strewn ridge
that encloses the tarn hidden at its feet.

Now advance over stony ground and make for the R.
corner of the tarn, where a conspicuous boulder is poised
beside its outflow. This point unfolds a splendid near-view
of Craig y Cau, whose shattered front of buttresses, gullies
and grassy terraces all rise diagonally R. to peter out below
the skyline. On the extreme R. there is a stone shoot that
affords a quick descent to the tarn, but is not recommended in the reverse direction. The crags of this fine
pyramid are not a satisfactory playground for the rock
climber, but a difficult course exists on the face of the
Pencoed Pillar L., which is separated from the main cliff
by the fearsome Great Gully.

Continue the ascent by skirting the shore of the tarn and

Cadair Idris

Bwlch Llyn Bach →

Plate 202. TAL-Y-LLYN AND BEGINNING OF ROUTE 45

bear R. to join the well-worn route. Climb this track which later gains the crest of the precipices enclosing the cwm to the north, and keep to its crest while enjoying the extensive views towards Tal-y-llyn L., whose shimmering blue is occasionally glimpsed through gaps in the folds of the hills. Note also the terrific cliffs of Pen y Gadair across the tarn R., and Cwm Amarch engirdled by crags L., with beyond it the long sloping ridge of Mynydd Pencoed, then walk up to the cairn on Craig y Cau.

After a well-earned rest on this breezy top, continue the walk by descending to the col that joins this subsidiary peak to the main ridge of Cadair, and note in passing the head of the stone shoot R. already mentioned. Pen y Gadair now towers into the sky ahead and its sharp, rocky summit crowns the long ridge stretching to east and west. The track skirts the crags of this peak, but on attaining the ridge leave it and bear L. along the rim of the cwm that cradles Llyn y Gadair R. until the cairn at the end of Cyfrwy is reached. This is the best viewpoint for the appraisal of the tremendous terraced cliffs of Cadair and also for the long scree of the Foxes' Path L. It is, moreover, a safe place from which to observe the narrow broken ridge of Cyfrwy that falls to the conspicuous Table, once the scene of an accident to a well-known mountaineer, but since the ridge consists of loose and unreliable rock it is best left alone. Now return along the edge of the cliffs and climb to the summit of Pen y Gadair where there is plenty of shelter just below the cairn so that climbers can find a comfortable resting place on a cold and windy day.

When the atmosphere is clear the vast panorama of mountains, valleys, lakes and sea unfolded from this lofty perch is one of the finest in all Wales. The splendour of the northern arc discloses wide vistas of Cardigan Bay on the west, with glimpses of Barmouth at the mouth of the Mawddach Estuary, spanned by the famous bridge. The whole of Snowdonia may be seen far to the north

Stone Shoot

Craig y Cau

Pencoed Pillar

Llyn y Cau

Plate 203. ROUTE 45

Cyfrwy →

← Stone Shoot

Pen–y–Gadair →

Cwm y Cau →

Plate 204. Route 45—Upper Section seen from Craig y Cau

Cyfrwy — Ridge — Harlech Dome — Snowdon — ←Table

Plate 205. ROUTE 45

beyond the intervening heights of the Harlech Dome, where Diffwys and the Rhinogs lead the eye to Yr Wyddfa R. The rounded summit of Rhobell Fawr is almost in line with the lonely Arennigs farther away on the open moorland, while to the north-east Bala Lake and the Arans are prominent on the extreme R. The southern arc is less spectacular and the eye is drawn to Plynlimon which may be perceived crowning the swelling moorland horizon.

Climbers who have arranged for a car to meet them at Llyn Gwernan will descend the mountain by the Foxes' Path, which leaves the ridge some little distance to the east of the summit. They will pass both Llyn y Gadair and Llyn y Gafr on the way down and obtain remarkable retrospects of the long line of precipices in the late afternoon light. Those making for the Youth Hostel at Kings will take a westerly course along the ridge and descend at the saddle of Rhiw Gwredydd, or if preferred continue to Tyrau Mawr and skirt Craig Las to reach the road. Those who wish to return to Tal-y-llyn, however, have four routes open to them: they can return the way they came, but may shorten the walk by descending the stone shoot at the col; they can diverge R. at this point and traverse the crest of Cwm Amarch, walking thence down steep grass slopes past a little shimmering tarn direct to the lake; they can stroll eastwards along the first section of the ridge, but bear R. before reaching Mynydd Moel and then go down a rather indistinct track beside a dilapidated stone wall to join the route of ascent above the trees; and they can continue along the entire length of the summit ridge to the end of Gau Graig, traversing Mynydd Moel *en route*, and thereafter descend carefully through the crags to the road near the top of the pass R. The latter is undoubtedly the finest course, with the Arans prominent on the north-eastern skyline all the way.

334

Plate 206. ROUTE 45. THE MAWDDACH ESTUARY FROM CYFRWY

Plate 207. ROUTE 45—PEN Y GADAIR AND THE FOXES' PATH FROM CYFRWY

THE HARLECH DOME

Y Llethr	2,475 feet
Diffwys	2,462 feet
Rhinog Fawr	2,362 feet
Rhinog Fach	2,333 feet
Moel Penolau	2,046 feet
Craig Ddrwg	1,937 feet
Llawllech	1,930 feet
Moel y Blithcwm	1,804 feet
Carreg y Saeth	1,442 feet
Bwlch Tyddiad	1,294 feet
Ewlch Drws Ardudwy	1,250 feet

MAP 9
THE HARLECH DOME

THIS is the long backbone of hills almost parallel with the coast of Mid-Wales which extends from north to south for a distance of some six miles. Moel Penolau stands like a sentinel overlooking Tremadoc Bay in the north, while Llawllech forms the southern outpost of the ridge above Barmouth Bay. Y Llethr dominates the whole chain at an altitude of 2,475 feet, but is only thirteen feet higher than its close neighbour, Diffwys. However, the two peaks which appeal more strongly to the climber are Rhinog Fawr and Rhinog Fach, because in clear weather the former reveals the whole of Snowdonia to the north, and both of them cradle a number of wildly situated tarns. Rhinog Fawr is bounded on the north by the famous Roman Steps and by the wild pass of Bwlch Tyddiad, while the two peaks are separated by the desolate pass of Bwlch Drws Ardudwy. Moreover, they are some of the most rugged hills in the country and are strewn with large boulders and scree which, to make matters worse for the climber, are literally covered with waist-high heather.

Rhinog Fawr is easily ascended from the farm at the end of the narrow road beyond Llyn Cwmbychan, which, with careful driving, may be reached by car from the village of Llanbedr situated on the main thoroughfare between Harlech and Barmouth. Rhinog Fach is most accessible from the farm of Maesygarnedd, which stands at the head of Nant Col and is the centre of the vast amphitheatre formed by the two mountains. It may also be reached by car from the same village by driving over four miles of a narrow, twisting and much gated road. Strong walkers who are able to arrange transport would do best to drive to the latter place early in the morning, climb and traverse the two peaks, having arranged for their car to meet them at the farm beyond Llyn Cwmbychan in the evening. This comprehensive but tough route discloses the finest scenery in the district, and includes Llyn Perfeddau, Llyn Hywel and Llyn y Bi during the ascent, and Llyn Du, Gloywlyn and Llyn Cwmbychan, as well as the Roman Steps, on the way down.

Route 46 The Roman Steps and Rhinog Fawr The delightful sylvan Vale of Artro extends from Llanbedr to Llyn Cwmbychan, a quiet little tarn overhung by the rocks of Craig y Saeth R., whence the rough hill road continues to the farm. Turn R. over a bridge and follow the path through a coppice to emerge eventually on the craggy hill-side. At this point it is necessary to keep a sharp look-out for the Roman Steps, which lead ultimately to Bwlch Tydd-iad, because it is easy to miss their longest and best stretch as the path runs below them for some distance It begins on the other side of a stone wall and lies immediately beneath the crags enclosing the south side of the narrow defile, According to tradition the steps were constructed by the Romans to facilitate the ascent and descent of their sentries, but they are now ascribed to mediaeval times.

Now walk along this ancient promenade to the crest of the pass and observe the featureless nature of the extensive moor of Trawsfynydd. Hereabouts the rugged spurs of Rhinog Fawr overhang too precipitously for their safe ascent, and it is better to go back until a weakness in the form of a steep watercourse appears in these ramparts. This is the easiest point at which to begin the toilsome ascent. Climb slowly and carefully between the large boulders almost hidden by heather for perhaps 300 feet and then edge round a big buttress to reach Llyn Du. This desolate sheet of water occupies a striking situation on the northern flanks of Rhinog Fawr and is enclosed on the south by broken precipices which extend upwards to the top of the mountain. Scale the ridge at the west corner of the tarn to eventually attain the two cairns on the summit of this peak.

When the atmosphere is clear this relatively close and lofty coign of vantage opens up a remarkable prospect of Snowdonia to the north. The Moelwyns are the nearest, with glimpses of Cnicht L. and Moel Siabod R., while Moel

Hebog is prominent to the north-west, with much of the Nantlle Ridge L. Between these two groups of hills Snowdon and its satellites stand supreme, and R. of them and above Gallt y Wenallt there is a distant glimpse of Y Garn and Glyder Fawr. The Rivals are conspicuous to the west beyond the blue of Tremadoc Bay, and the Arennigs appear across the moorland to the north-east. Due east this aspect of the Arans is disappointing, whereas to the south and above Y Llethr the long line of cliffs supporting Cadair Idris rivet the gaze.

The quickest descent would appear to be in a direct line with the glittering blue of Gloywlyn far below, but since the intervening slopes are littered with large boulders hidden by deep heather, the walk down involves many detours and may be rather fatiguing. The lake is cradled in a shallow basin to the south-east of Craig y Saeth and, as it is a favourite with local anglers, there is a well-trodden path from its shore right down to the farm in the valley.

Bwlch Tyddiad

Plate 208. ROUTE 46—THE ROMAN STEPS

Y Llethr →   Rhinog Fach →   Bwlch Drws Ardudwy →   Rhinog Fawr →

Plate 209.   Routes 46 and 47—The Rhinogs from the East

Y Llethr

Rhinog Fach

Llyn Perfeddau

Llyn Hywel

Plate 210. Route 47 seen from the Summit of Rhinog Fawr

RHINOG FACH

Route 47. Nantcol and Rhinog Fach. Climbers who drive from Llanbedr to Nantcol will be surprised at the number of gates that have to be opened and shut before the farm of Maes y garnedd is reached. The narrow and sinuous hill road threading this valley gives access to perhaps a dozen farms which may account for these several closures, but the last time I passed this way I counted them and made the number only nine, so probably others had fallen into decay.

Leave the farm and take a direct line for Y Llethr in the south-east, but keep L. of its spur to reach Llyn Perfeddau which lies to the north of this mountain. It is cradled in a grassy hollow and reveals a fine view of Rhinog Fach, whose precipitous front towers into the sky to the north-east. On deserting the tarn take a direct line for it and climb a stony gully that peters out on the shore of Llyn Hywel. This tarn occupies the floor of a deep hollow between Y Llethr and Rhinog Fach, and as it is wide open to the prevailing south-westerly winds it can be a wild and boisterous place. The scene is on the grand scale and one of the most awe-inspiring in this group of hills. To the north the broken crags supporting the summit of Rhinog Fach rise literally from a sea of boulders and scree; to the south the steep ridge of Y Llethr runs up to the skyline and its sharp edge consists of gigantic slabs of rock lying end-on at an angle of forty-five degrees, while its base sinks down into the depths of the lake.

The col between the two peaks is the key to their ascent, and to attain it walk first to the south side of the tarn and then scale a gully that slants up a break in the slabs of rock. There are ample hand- and foot-holds and on reaching the skyline a wall is encountered, from which note the rippling surface of Llyn y Bi some distance below. A track runs beside this wall and gives access to most of the summits crowning this long line of hills, so if bound for Y Llethr

345

Plate 211. Nantcol—Route 47 starts here

Rhinog Fach

Bwlch Drws Ardudwy

Maes-y-garnedd

Rhinog Fawr

turn R., or if for Rhinog Fach turn L. where the wall terminates at the summit cairn.

The panorama unfolded from this mountain top is not dissimilar from that of its neighbour, save that the latter, which is twenty-nine feet higher, obscures a part of the view of Snowdonia. Begin the descent by walking along the declining summit ridge, on which the path peters out at the small cairn at its terminus, and look down the dizzy precipices overlooking Bwlch Drws Ardudwy far below. Do not attempt to descend them, but bear L. and scramble carefully down the western flanks of the peak, making for the tiny pool of Llyn Cwmhosan, whence continue through boulders and heather until the pass is reached and then turn L. to follow the stream down to Nantcol.

Plate 212. ROUTE 47—RHINOG FACH FROM LLYN HYWEL

Plate 213. ROUTE 47—SLABS OF Y LLETHR

Y Llethr

Rhinog Fach

Llyn Hywel

Plate 214. RETROSPECT OF ROUTE 47

THE ARENNIGS

ARENNIG FAWR	.	.	2,800 feet
ARENNIG FACH	.	.	2,264 feet
CRAIG Y BYCHAN	.	.	2,221 feet
MOEL YMENYN	.	.	1,801 feet
LLYN ARENNIG FACH	.	.	1,400 feet
LLYN ARENNIG FAWR	.	.	1,326 feet

THE Arennigs are two conspicuous hills dominating the barren stretches of moorland in the northern corner of Mid-Wales. Arennig Fawr is the higher and more shapely eminence and attains an altitude of 2,800 feet above sea level, while Arennig Fach is a mere rounded hump on the heathery wilderness to the north of it, and is 2,264 feet high. Both of these mountains may be ascended without difficulty from any direction, but the latter is of no interest to the climber. The former rises immediately to the south of Arennig Station, eight miles from Bala and thirteen and a half from Ffestiniog. Since the station is on the 1,135-foot contour, the ascent involves only 1,665 feet of climbing.

The most direct route lies up a wide grassy hollow dappled with scree, whence the undulating ridge leads straight to the broad backbone of the summit, which falls to the south-east where it is embellished with a number of strange little peaks. This affords a favourite descent for those who traverse the mountain on the way from Arennig Station to the village of Llanwchllyn, a distance of eleven miles.

The only interesting and revealing ascent of Arennig Fawr involves a considerable detour to the south-east and skirts the shores of Llyn Arennig Fawr at a height of 1,326 feet. This lonely tarn lies immediately below a number of outcropping buttresses which are the occasional resort of the rock climber. From the southern end of the lake a rough ridge leads to a grassy plateau that preludes the final slopes to the strange cairn on the summit of the mountain.

351

MAP 10
THE ARENNIGS

Route 48. Bala, Llyn Arennig Fawr and Arennig Fawr.
Leave Bala by the main highway to Ffestiniog, but when
half a mile from the town turn L. at the fork which is the
old Arennig road. Pass a gate L. that gives access to the
open moor, where the white walls of a few tree-girt farm-
steads afford some relief to the barren prospect. Continue
ahead across the brown and green wilderness until the
cottages clustered round Arennig Station come into view.
During the greater part of this journey Arennig Fawr
dominates the scene, but the mountain disappears behind
a craggy spur on the approach to the hamlet.

Park the car near the station and walk back along the
road to a corrugated iron building R., then pass through a
gate on to the open moor. Follow a rather indistinct sheep
track round the lower slopes of Gelli-deg R. until the
glimmering surface of Llyn Arennig Fawr appears ahead.
Note the terraced outcrops of rock overhanging its south
side, which are the occasional resort of the rock climber,
but keep L. round its shore. This remote tarn occupies
one of the wildest and most desolate situations hereabouts
and is in consequence seldom visited. Go ahead until its
outflow is reached, where some piers and the dam constructed long ago confirm the conversion of the lake into a
reservoir. Continue southwards and make for a rough ridge
that is supported by some bold terraced buttresses. Climb
the steep slopes L. and on attaining its crest Arennig Fawr
is revealed on the western skyline. Now walk across the
grassy plateau in a direct line with the cairn and ascend the
last slopes to its summit.

The first object to attract the eye on this lofty peak will be
the monument erected to commemorate the death of eight
gallant Americans who crashed in their Flying Fortress on
August 4th, 1943, their machine having collided with the
rocks a few feet below the western side of the summit. Then

Arennig Fawr

Plate 215. ARENNIG FAWR FROM THE EAST

scan the vast panorama which on a clear day is very extensive owing to the isolated position of the mountain. Snowdon dominates the numerous prominent peaks on the north-western skyline; a glimpse of Bala Lake is disclosed to the south-east and is backed by the Berwyns; the twin tops of the Arans appear almost due south, with Rhobell Fawr on R., the latter being capped by the long cliff-line of Cadair Idris; while the circle is completed in the south-west by the ridge of high hills crowned by Y Llethr.

Rest awhile to enjoy these revealing views and then begin the descent by walking due north along the broad backbone that extends below the summit. Bear R. to reach the rocky terminus of Craig yr Hyrddod which opens up a bird's-eye view of Llyn Arennig Fawr below to the east, and then enter the wide grassy hollow that leads direct to Arennig Station.

During this descent there are also spacious views of the new reservoir in the vast Tryweryn Valley below, whose impounded water is piped to Liverpool. It is now known as Llyn Celyn.

Plate 216   Route 48—Llyn Arennig Fawr

Plate 217. ROUTE 48—THE SUMMIT OF ARENNIG FAWR

THE ARANS

ARAN FAWDDWY	. .	2,970 feet
ARAN BENLLYN .	. .	2,901 feet
DRWS BACH	. .	2,500 feet
DRYSGOL .	. .	2,397 feet
CAMDDWR .	. .	2,248 feet
CRAIG CWM-DU .	.	2,246 feet
CRAIG CYWARCH	.	2,100 feet
CRAIG TY-NANT .	.	2,010 feet
CREIGLYN DYFI .	.	1,900 feet
Y GRIBIN .	.	1,870 feet
HENGWM RIM	.	1,862 feet
BWLCH Y GROES.	.	1,790 feet
LLYN LLIWBRAN	.	1,550 feet
CRAIG Y GEIFR	.	1,500 feet
MOEL DU .	. .	1,500 feet

THE ARANS

THE rocky summit of Aran Fawddwy crowns the highest ridge south of Snowdonia: it attains an altitude of 2,970 feet, and is thus forty-three feet higher than Cadair Idris; sixty feet higher than Pen y Fan, the dominating peak of the Brecon Beacons; and 501 feet higher than Plynlimon. The ridge is one and a half miles in length and Aran Fawddwy stands at its southern end, the northern out-post being Aran Benllyn, which is 2,901 feet above sea level and overlooks Bala Lake.

These hills do not present an inviting aspect when viewed from the south and west and appear merely to crown a vast area of billowy moorland. If, however, Aran Benllyn is seen from Bala Lake its precipitous eastern front is dis-closed, and this alone will tempt the mountaineer to climb it. On closer inspection this line of black cliffs, flecked with white quartz and seamed with gullies, will be found to support almost the full length of the ridge. The only break is at its centre, where a grassy spur extends eastwards, its lower slopes cradling the circular tarn of Creiglyn Dyfi, which is the lonely birthplace of the River Dovey.

Both of these peaks may be reached easily from any point to the north, south and west of them, but their eastern flanks are not so accessible. Those who wish to climb them from this direction may do so by walking first towards Bwlch y Groes, and then turning westwards along one of its subsidiary valleys. The most interesting ascent, how-ever, is that of Aran Fawddwy by way of the remote ham-let of Abercywarch, which lies a mile to the north of Dinas Mawddwy. Here a narrow farm road diverges L. of the highway and rises sharply between the cottages. It then threads a valley patterned with green fields and watered by the Afon Cywarch and, taking a north-westerly direction, ends at the farm of Caeperis, which is situated immediately

MAP 11
THE ARANS

below the frowning cliffs of Craig Cywarch. A footbridge marks the commencement of the best route to Aran Fawddwy, and ascends over grass before joining the old peat track that rises gradually for over two miles and peters out in the bogs at the foot of Drysgol. The latter is an undulating, grassy spur extending eastwards from the reigning peak, and its crest is traversed to the base of the gullied precipices that rise directly to the conspicuous cairn on its summit.

Route 49. Dinas Mawddwy and Drysgol. Leave Dinas Mawddwy by the road to Bwlch y Groes and note the sparkling cascades of the Dyfi R. On reaching Aber Cywarch turn L. and on emerging from the hedgerows beyond the cottages cross the green strath to Caeperis. The farm is splendidly situated amid a circle of green hills, but on the west is overhung by the black, forbidding cliffs of Craig Cywarch. Cross the bridge and follow the path where a line of trees marks the direction of the old peat track. This rises at an easy gradient for two miles and is cushioned with springy turf and fringed with golden sedge. Plod along steadily and meanwhile note how the floor of Hengwm L. recedes with every step until at the end of the path it is nearly 2,000 feet below. Observe also L. on the other side of it the magnificent buttresses and gullies of Craig Cywarch, which in the last decade have been explored by rock climbers.

Now keep to the wire fence across the maze of bog and later bear R. for some outcropping rocks where a charming little pool lies on the level end of the spur. This point discloses for the first time on this ascent the shattered front of Aran Fawddwy to the west, together with the cliffs of Aran Benllyn above the grassy spur in the centre of the ridge, as well as Creiglyn Dyfi far below held firmly in the grip of the hillside by a bulge in the grassy slope.

Drysgol narrows considerably as it bends round the head of Hengwm and at one spot, where a gully falls precipitously to the south, it is so narrow that the edge has given way. This coign of vantage is a good one for the appraisal of the shattered front of Aran Fawddwy, riven with gullies and surmounted by a cairn which is clearly silhouetted against the sky. These gullies are the occasional playground of rock-climbing initiates.

Continue the walk past the cairn on Drws Bach, erected in 1961 by the RAF (SAC Michael Robert Aspin of the RAF Mountain Rescue was killed by lightning here), cross the narrow ridge and make for the L. corner of the precipices. Turn R. and climb the broken rocks that rise to the first cairn, or if preferred avoid them by going farther L. to pick up a sheep track that mounts over grass. On attaining the crest of the ridge the reigning peak is disclosed on the skyline about half a mile to the north. Make your way through the chaotically arranged boulders and on reaching the summit cairn sit down to eat lunch and admire the spacious panorama.

Since the Arans are the most easterly peaks in Mid-Wales it follows that the most interesting views are round the western arc. Cadair Idris is seen almost end-on with the Harlech Dome R. Then come the peaks of Snowdonia and the isolated Arennigs that rise from the swelling moorland. Aran Benllyn is prominent at the end of the summit ridge, with R. Creiglyn Dyfi below, beyond which rise the vast moors of the Berwyns.

Climbers who are making the traverse of this group will continue along the ridge to Aran Benllyn and then walk downhill all the way to Llanuwchllyn and eventually to Bala.

In recent years Craig Cywarch has been explored more fully by members of the Mountain Club, who, in 1960, started to build and equip a Cottage now known as Bryn Hafod, which was opened in October, 1965. There is ample camping space nearby and cars may be parked on the adjacent Common. In due course accommodation will be available in the Cottage for visiting mountaineers, by arrangement.

Plate 218. CRAIG CYWARCH SEEN FROM ROUTE 49

Plate 219. ROUTE 49—ARAN BENLLYN FROM DRYSGOL

Plate 220.   ROUTE 49—CREIGLYN DYFI—BIRTHPLACE OF THE RIVER DOVEY

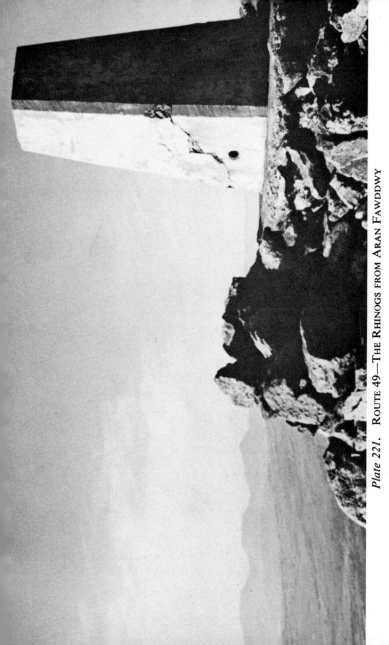

Plate 221. ROUTE 49—THE RHINOGS FROM ARAN FAWDDWY

Plate 222. ROUTE 49—THE RIDGE TO ARAN BENLLYN

PLYNLIMON

PEN PLYNLIMON FAWR . . . 2,468 feet

MAP 12
PLYNLIMON

PLYNLIMON is one of the three chief mountains of Wales, the others, as already noted, being Snowdon and Cadair Idris. The summit of Pen Plynlimor. Fawr is 2,468 feet above sea level, but since its environs are already lofty the mountain lacks the imposing appearance of many lesser peaks. The vast plateau extends from south-west to north-east and consists of grit and shale overlaid with coarse grass and bog; in fact satirists have described it as a "sodden weariness". However, this great dome is the source of the rivers Severn, Wye and Rheidol, and its slopes also give birth to several lesser noteworthy streams. It was Owen Glendower's lair in 1401, whence he sallied forth to harry the land.

There are two popular routes to the summit: that from Dyffryn Castell Hotel is longer and traverses three and a half miles of a broad gradually rising ridge; that from the Farm of Eisteddfa Gurig is about half the distance and threads a wild valley to an abandoned lead mine, to rise thereafter direct to the cairn on the summit. Some years ago both routes were well marked by a continuous line of stakes driven into the ground, which in mist were a sure guide, for they ran right up to the top of the mountain. But although those on the route from Eisteddfa Gurig are still in existence, those from the hotel were removed during the Second World War and have not been replaced.

Climbers who visit this region solely to ascend Plynlimon could not do better than stay at Dyffryn Castell Inn, which has ten bedrooms and a bathroom, and is right on the spot for the walk. There is a larger hotel in Ponterwyd, some two miles distant, and another at the Devil's Bridge that is four miles away. The latter has the advantage of proximity to the Rheidol Valley, a magnificently wooded basin immediately opposite, which affords charming walks for those who come to explore the district. There is accommodation at Eisteddfa Gurig, which is on the main road about three miles beyond Dyffryn Castell.

371

Route 50. From the Devil's Bridge. The drive to the foot of Plynlimon is pleasant and by taking the R. fork at Tyn-y-ffordd the road attains the 1,005-foot contour and hereabouts opens up the only good view of the mountain. Thereafter it descends in graceful curves, eventually to merge with the main highway just short of Dyffryn Castell, where there is a car park beside the hotel. Thence the road rises at an easy gradient along a wide, desolate valley, with the lofty grass ridge leading to the peak L., but the monotony of the landscape is relieved here and there by a few larches, which, however, disappear all too soon. and by extensive spruce plantations away to the R. Eisteddfa Gurig stands at a bend on the crest of the pass and cars may be parked in the farmyard. A conspicuous notice board on the gate clearly defines the shorter route of ascent to the cairn.

Pass through two gates R. of *Dyffryn Castell* and then bear L. to climb the steep grassy slopes of the ridge immediately overhead. On attaining its crest bear R. at an easier gradient and keep the valley in view R. while ascending gradually over grass, heather and bracken for about two miles. Avoid the tremendous bogs L. and always keep to the higher ground, with Plynlimon ahead slightly L. until the shorter route is encountered, whence follow the stakes to its summit.

When compared with the views from other peaks in Wales, that from Plynlimon is disappointing owing to the immensity of the moorland plateau in the vicinity, which seemingly diminishes its real height. The only mountains of note in the extensive panorama are Cadair Idris and the Arans away to the north.

Eisteddfa Gurig stands on the 1,358-foot contour and the ascent to the summit of Plynlimon involves a climb of only 1,110 feet. Pass through the farmyard and follow the disused cart-track all the way to the lead mine, first beside a playful stream with chattering cascades here and there, and then R. through great expanses of boggy moorland. Pick

Plate 223. PLYNLIMON FROM THE SOUTH

up the stakes at the lead mine and climb steadily beside them to the cairn. There is absolutely nothing to relieve the monotony of the landscape on this route: no trees to break the skyline, no colourful flowers to carpet the wayside, no birds to charm both ear and eye, just the green and brown of grass and bog. Incidentally, both routes are much pleasanter going after a dry spell.

A correspondent who knows this region intimately suggests the following alternative approaches which he says are more interesting.

Drive or walk from Ponterwyd past Nantymoch reservoir to the small holding of Brynybeddau, whence proceed up the remote valley of the Rheidol. One of three routes can then be chosen, depending on time and inclination:

1. Turn R. for Llyn Llygad Rheidol and ascend through grassy crags to the summit of Plynlimon Fawr.
2. Turn up Cwm Gwann to the top of Pen Plynlimon-wstle and walk along the ridge to the dominating summit.
3. Follow the stream almost to Llyn Bugeilyn and then attain the ridge to walk back, passing the source of the River Severn en route.

Plate 224. ROUTE 50

Dyffryn Castell

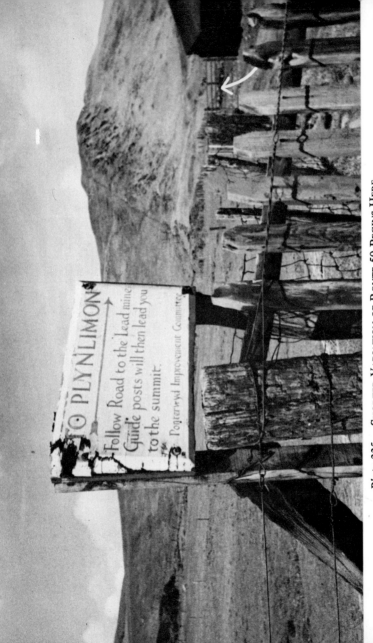

TO PLYNLIMON

Follow Road to the Lead mine.
Guide posts will then lead you
to the summit.

Pegterwyd Improvement Committee

Plate 225. SHORTER VARIATION OF ROUTE 50 BEGINS HERE

Plate 226. ROUTE 50—EISTEDDFA GURIG

THE BLACK MOUNTAINS

WAUN FACH	. . .	2,660 feet
PEN Y GADER FAWR	. .	2,624 feet
PEN Y MANLLWYN	. .	2,500 feet
PEN ALLT MAWR	. .	2,360 feet
PEN TRUMAU	. .	2,320 feet
TWYN TAL-Y-CEFN	. .	2,303 feet
CHWAREL Y FAN .	. .	2,228 feet
PEN Y BEACON	. .	2,219 feet
PEN GLOCH-Y-PIBWR	.	2,210 feet
MYNYDD LLYSIAU	. .	2,173 feet
BLACK HILL	. . .	2,102 feet
PENTWYNGLAS	. . .	2,115 feet

Plate 227. The Black Mountains from Skirrid Fawr

MAP 13
THE BLACK MOUNTAINS

THE BLACK MOUNTAINS

THE Black Mountains cover an area of about eighty square miles to the north of Abergavenny. They consist largely of bleak, whale-back ridges running from south-east to north-west, and are dominated by the Gadair Ridge, which is crowned by Waun Fach, the highest peak in the whole group. Strangely enough all of them are about the same altitude, and rise just above the 2,000-foot contour.

Three long valleys penetrate the fastnesses of the range: the Vale of Ewyas is the longest and most beautiful and is graced by the venerable ruin of Llanthony Priory. All the valleys follow roughly parallel lines in a north-westerly direction and terminate in the shadow of a broken ridge which connects all four of the main ridges.

These ridges and valleys are excellent walking country and a variety of routes may be worked out from the one-inch Ordnance Survey Map and in clear weather followed with little difficulty. But it is important to know some of the landmarks with certainty, owing to the very slight differences in height of a few of the peaks. This approximation in altitude is not always apparent unless they are seen from afar and a case in point is that of the dominating Gadair Ridge where the difference in height between Waun Fach and Pen y Gadair Fawr is only thirty-six feet. When traversing the ridge this is not very clear, save perhaps from the latter top, but is quite apparent when observed from the highest parts of the Allt Mawr Ridge, over three miles to the south. When making the following ascent these features are worthy of note, and on attaining Waun Fach its summit will reveal the immensity of the range and perhaps induce the climber to make a more detailed exploration.

Plate 228.   ROUTE 51—Y GRIB LEADING TO PEN Y MANLLWYN

Route 51. The Gadair Ridge. A convenient starting point for this ascent is the sequestered hamlet of Pen y genffordd which stands at the highest point of the road, 1,060 feet, between Crickhowell and Talgarth. Climbers who approach it from the south will note the lofty ridge of Pen Allt Mawr which hems in the valley R. almost all the way from Crickhowell. A reference to the map will show that Y Grib is the key to this route, and the foot of its ridge is reached by following an old farm track which passes round the north side of Castell Dinas. Advance along it for about half a mile and then take a direct line for its conspicuous spur seen on the skyline ahead. On attaining its narrow crest, which is embellished here and there by outcropping rocks, climb its sharp undulations and make for Pen y Manllwyn, a broad grassy top at the northern extremity of the Gadair Ridge. Then turn R. and walk for just over a mile in a southerly direction to Waun Fach, the reigning peak of the group, which does not boast a cairn but displays only an O.S. Triangulation Station.

This lofty viewpoint unfolds an extensive panorama, in which the Brecon Beacons will draw the eye to the distant south-west, but the nearer whale-back ridges of the group are so immense that they obscure the deep valleys of the range. It also reveals the strange hump of Pen y Gadair Fawr over a mile to the south-east and its summit, crowned by a large cairn, may be reached by picking one's way carefully across the intervening boggy ground.

Plate 229.   THE BRECON BEACONS FROM ROUTE 51

Plate 230.   ROUTE 51—PEN Y GADAIR AND THE SUGAR LOAF FROM WAUN FACH

THE BRECON BEACONS

PEN Y FAN .	. . .	2,907 feet
CORN DU .	. . .	2,863 feet
CRIBYN	. . .	2,608 feet

MAP 14
THE BRECON BEACONS

THE BRECON BEACONS

THESE mountains form a compact and shapely group that is situated about mid-way between the Black Mountains on the east and Fforest Fawr and Carmarthen Fan on the west. The principal summits are Pen y Fan, 2,907 feet, Corn Du, 2,863 feet, and Cribyn, 2,608 feet. Pen y Fan is the loftiest peak in South Wales and is a conspicuous object when seen from afar. The group is particularly attractive when viewed from the north, and the dominating peak assumes spectacular proportions when seen from the adjacent rib of Bryn Teg; it rises five miles to the south-west of Brecon.

The easiest and quickest way to traverse the Brecon Beacons is from the Storey Arms, which stands at a height of 1,440 feet on the crest of the pass carrying the main road south from Brecon to Merthyr Tydfil. Mere peak-baggers may be satisfied with this short ascent which involves less than 1,500 feet of climbing, but those who wish to see the real beauty of the group will miss much of it by doing so, and if they are also interested in photography and prefer, as they should, the most favourable lighting throughout, then they will follow the route described and illustrated herein.

The only snag for those without transport is that the complete circuit is a long one based upon Brecon and involves between twelve and fifteen miles of walking, depending upon such diversions as are made to toy with a camera. It is possible to drive due south from the town for three miles to a place where there is space for parking a car, and this would reduce the walking distance to perhaps seven miles. To reach this spot cross the bridge over the River Usk and then turn L. off the highway at a church; the road is narrow but well surfaced and turns R. at a school, thereafter to rise gradually in a southerly direction to end near a disused farm at Cantref.

Plate 231. ROUTE 52—PEN Y FAN FROM CANTREF

Route 52. Cantref and Pen y Fan. Proceed along the rough road which soon deteriorates into a stony cart-track, cross a brook fringed with trees, and continue ahead for about a mile in the direction of Cwm Cynwyn. Pass through a gate R. and ascend the slopes of the grassy ridge, pass some small pools on its crest with the cliffs of Pen y Fan R., and take a direct line for the steep rib of Bryn Teg which culminates in the peak of Cribyn. Note the disused cart-track which contours across the slopes of Cwm Cynwyn L., and then tackle the sharp ridge ahead. This is continuously steep and the going is hard for the time being, but on reaching its summit the rewards are immense; for the full stature of Pen y Fan is now revealed in all its grandeur, its precipitous front seamed with gullies hundreds of feet long and ribbed with grass and moss to afford a picture of mountain beauty. Farther L. the ground sweeps down to a little col and then rises again to the crowning peak of the range, beneath which the Afon Cynrig has its source. Now descend to the col and climb to the summit of Pen y Fan, meanwhile noting R. its flat top supported by blocks of red sandstone lying end-on and poised above the innumerable layers of the same rock which alternate with successive bands of bright red earth.

The small summit plateau carries an O.S. Triangulation Station and opens up an extensive panorama in which the vast bulk of the Black Mountains appear to the east and the peaks of Fforest Fawr lead the eye to Carmarthen Fan in the west. Now continue the walk to Corn Du, whose long summit ridge is rimmed with crags R. and reveals far below the circular Llyn Cwm-llwch. Then go back to Pen y Fan and descend the grassy spur of Cefn Cwm-llwch to Allt Ddu, whence bear R. and walk down to the point of departure.

Bryn Teg

Plate 232.   THE STEEPEST ASCENT ON ROUTE 52

Pen-y-Fan

Plate 233. Route 52 from Cribyn

Plate 234. ROUTE 52—CORN DU FROM PEN Y FAN

Plate 235. ROUTE 52—LLYN CWM-LLWCH FROM CORN DU

INDEX

ABER, 249
Aber Cywarch, 362
Aber Falls, 249
Abergavenny, 26, 382
Aberglaslyn Pass, 292
Adam and Eve, 162
Afon Cywarch, 359
    Colwyn, 288
    Cynrig, 392
    Glaslyn, 265, 281, 288
    Lledr, 271
    Llugwy, 168, 220
    Llyn Edno, 265
Amphitheatre, 224
Anglesey, 186, 315
Aran Benllyn, 359
    Fawddwy, 359
    Yr, 92, 100
Ardudwy, 339
Arennig Fach, 351
    Fawr, 351, 353
Arthog, 326
Artro, 340
Aryg, Yr, 249

BALA, 24, 326, 353, 359
Barmouth, 25, 330
Beddgelert, 23, 288, 292
Bera Mawr, 249
Berwyns, 355
Bethesda, 22, 245
Betws-y-coed, 21, 271
Black Ladders, 234
Black Mountains, 382

Blaenau Ffestiniog, 283
Boots, 14
Brecon, 26, 390
Brecon Beacons, 387
Bristly Ridge, 152, 168
Bryn Teg, 390
Bwlch y Brecan, 186
    Caseg-fraith, 168
    Coch, 68
    Cwmbrwynog, 116
    Cwm-llan, 100
    Drosbern, 308
    Drws Ardudwy, 339 347
    Glas, 78
    y Groes, 359
    Gylfin, 298
    Main, 92, 100
    y Moch, 68
    Rhiwgwrefydd, 323
    y Saethau, 68, 86
    Tryfan, 152, 164
    Tyddiad, 339

CADAIR IDRIS, 323
Caeperis, 362
Caernarvon, 288, 308
Cantilever, 152
Cantref, 390, 392
Cardigan Bay, 294, 330
Capel Curig, 23, 174, 204, 253
Carmarthen Fan, 390
Carneddau, 200
Carnedd Ddafydd, 234

Carnedd Llywelyn, 220, 245, 249
    Ugain, 72
    y Filiast, 135
Carreg y Saeth, 337
Castell Dinas, 384
Castle of the Winds, 152
Centres, 21
Climbers' Club, 20
Clogwyn Du'r Arddu, 116
    Marchnad, 287
    Mawr, 204
    Station, 124
    y Person, 134
Cnicht, 265, 272, 277
Corn Du, 390
Crafnant, Llyn, 204
Craig Cywarch, 362
    Cwm-bychan, 117
    Cwm Silyn, 298
    Ddrwg, 337
    Eigiau, 200
    Las, 334
    Llugwy, 234
    Llyn, 323
    Wen, 208
    Ysgafn, 283
Craig y Bere, 315
    Bychan, 351
    Cau, 326, 328
    Saeth, 340
    yr Hyrddod, 355
    yr Ysfa, 220
Creigiau Gleision, 208
Creiglyn Dyfi, 359
Cricieth, 308
Croesor, 265, 277, 281
Crib Goch, 66, 68
    y Ddysgl, 68
Cribyn, 390
Crickhowell, 26, 384
Cross Foxes, 326
Cwm Amarch, 334
Cwm Brwynog, 116
    Clogwyn, 108

Croesor, 271
Cynwyn, 392
Dyli, 68
Eigiau, 224
Glas, 129
Idwal, 146
Llafar, 245
Silyn, 298
Tryfan, 168
y Cau, 328
y Llan, 92
Cwm-cloch, 292
Cyfrwy, 326, 330
Cyfyng Falls, 260

DEINIOLEN, 186
Devil's Bridge, 25, 371, 372
    Kitchen, 138, 198
Diffwys, 339
Dinas, Llyn, 288
    Mawddwy, 24, 362
    Mot, 129
Dog Lakes, 265, 271
Dolgellau, 24, 326
Dolwyddelan, 254, 271
Dovey, River, 359
Drum, 200
Drws Bach, 358
    y-coed, 298
Dyffryn Castell, 371, 372
Dyfi, River, 362
Drysgol, 362

EISTEDDFA GURIG, 371, 372
Elen, Yr, 224, 245, 249
Elephant Mountain, 298
Elidir Fawr, 186
Equipment, 11
Esgair Felen, 182
Ewyas, Vale of, 382

FFESTINIOG, 283

Fforest Fawr, 390
Ffynnon Caseg, 245, 249
      Lloer, 234
      Llugwy, 220, 224
Foel Fras, 249
    Goch, 190
    Grach, 249
    Rudd, 315
Foxes' Path, 326, 330

GADAIR RIDGE, 382, 384
Gau Craig, 334
Gallt y Wenallt, 341
    yr Ogof, 174
Garnedd Goch, 308
Garn, Y, 190, 198
    Y II, 302
Garth Bridge, 47
Gladstone Rock, 92
Glaslyn, 78, 80
Glendower, Owen, 371
Glossary, 27
Gloywlyn, 339
Glyder Fach, 152
    Fawr, 138
Great Slab, Cwm Silyn, 308
Gribin, Y, Ogwen, 146
    Snowdon, 92
Gwynant Valley, 265, 288

HARLECH, 25, 308
    Dome, 337
Hay, 26
Heather Terrace, 158, 166
Heights of Peaks, 36
Helyg, 168, 220
Hengwm, 362
Holyhead Road, 174
Horseshoe, Snowdon, 60, 66

IDWAL, CWM, 140, 146
    Llyn, 140
    Slabs, 140, 199

LAST NAIL IN THE HORSESHOE,
  68

Llanbedr, 25, 339
Llanberis, 23
    Pass, 124
    Path, 124
Llanthony Abbey, 382
Lledr Valley, 271
Llanuwechllyn, 351, 363
Llawllech, 339
Llechog, 106
Lliwedd, 86
Llwytmor, 249
Llyn Arennig Fawr, 351, 353
    Bochlwyd, 152
    y Biswail, 271
    Caseg-fraith, 168
    Celyn, 355
    Clyd, 190
    Cowlyd, 208, 214
    Crafnant, 204
    Cwellyn, 108, 116
    Cwmbychan, 339
    Cwmllwch, 392
    Cwm Silyn, 298
    Cwmffynnon, 182
    Dinas, 288
    Du, 339
    Du'r Arddu, 116
    y Dywarchen, 317
    Edno, 265
    Eigiau, 220
    Ffynnon, Lloer 234
    Geirionnydd, 204
    Glas, 129
    Glaslyn, 78, 80
    Grwyne Fawr, 40
    Gwernan, 334
    Gwynant, 92
    Hywel, 339
    Idwal, 140
    Llagi, 272
    Llugwy, 224
    Llydaw, 68, 80, 92
    Lockwood, 178
    Nantlle Uchaf, 298
    Ogwen, 158, 234

Llyn Padarn, 125, 186
    Perfeddau, 339
    Peris, 198
    Stwlan, 283
    Teyrn, 80
    yr Adar, 271, 272
    y Bi, 339
      Cau, 326
      Cwn, 146
      Foel, 254, 260
      Gadair, 108, 326, 330
      Gafr, 334
Llynnau Mymbyr, 254
Llynnau Cwn, 271

MAESYGARNEDD, 339
Maps, 17
Marchlyn Bach, 186
      Mawr, 186
Matterhorn of Wales, 253
Mawddach Estuary, 326
Merthyr Tydfil, 390
Milestone Buttress, 158
Miners' Track, Glyders, 168, 178
Miners' Track, Snowdon, 80
Moel Cynghorion, 63
    Druman, 253
    Eilio, 63
    Hebog, 287, 288
    Lefn, 287
    Meirch, 265
    Penolau, 339
    Siabod, 253
    Ymenyn, 351
    y Blithcwm, 337
    yr Hydd, 253
      Ogof, 287
Moelwyn Bach, 283
      Mawr, 281
Mountain Photography, 41
Mynydd Drws-y-coed, 302
      Mawr, 315
      Moel, 334
      Perfedd, 186

Mynydd Talmignedd, 308

NAMELESS CWM, 146
    Peak, 174
Nant Col, 339, 345
    Ffrancon, 190
    Gwynant, 92
Nantlle, 308
    Ridge, 298
Nanmor, 265, 272
North Ridge of Tryfan, 158

OGWEN COTTAGE, 22, 138, 190, 198, 242
Ogwen Lake, 158, 234

PARSON'S NOSE, 129
Pencoed Pillar, 328
Pennant Horseshoe, 294
Pennant Valley, 308
Pen Allt Mawr, 382
    llithrig-y-wrach, 214
    Plynlimon Fawr, 369
    y Castell, 200
      Fan, 392, 394
      Gadair, 326, 330
        Fawr, 382
      Genffordd, 384
      Gwryd, 22, 168, 178, 182
      Pass, 22, 66, 68, 182
      Manllwyn, 384
      yr Helgi-du, 220
      Ole Wen, 242
Pillar of Elidir, 186
Pitt's Head, 106
Plas Cwm-llan, 92
Plynlimon, 369
Pont Cae'r-gors, 288
Ponterwyd, 371
Pyg Track, 78

RHEIDOL VALLEY, 371
Rhinog Fach, 339, 345
      Fawr, 339
Rhobell Fawr, 334

Rhyd-ddu, 106, 298
Rivals, 308
Rock Climbing, 19
Roman Steps, 339, 340
Routes, Notes on, 58
Royal Bridge, 254

SHOWELL STYLES, 277
Snowdon, 63, 254
        Horseshoe, 60, 66
        Ranger, 23, 116
Storey Arms, 26, 390
Sugar Loaf, 386

TALGARTH, 26, 384
Tal-y-braich, 220
    fan, 200
    llyn, 24, 326, 328
Tan-lan, 263
Tremadoc Bay, 339, 341
Tryfan, 158
    Scree Gully, 158
Trum y Ddysgl, 308

Trawsfynydd 326
Tryweryn Valley, 355
Tyrau Mawr, 334

USK, RIVER, 390

VALE OF ARTRO, 340
    Gwynant, 265, 288
    Nanmor, 265, 272

WATKIN PATH, 92
Waun Fach, 382

Y GARN, 190, 198
    II, 304
  Llethr, 339, 345
Yr Aran, 92, 100
  Aryg, 249
  Elen, 224, 245, 249
  Wyddfa, 68, 78
Ysgafell Wen, 271

ZIG-ZAGS, 68, 78

This ROUTE CARD is reproduced with the permission of the Chief Constable of Inverness-shire and is similar to others in use elsewhere in Scotland. The idea is sound and if adopted and used consistently by all climbers and walkers throughout our mountainous country it could be the means of facilitating any call for Mountain Rescue. I hope the English and Welsh Police will favour its use and distribute the Route Card widely wherever climbers and mountain walkers are lodged. It is, of course, most important that NO DIGRESSION is made from the stated route, otherwise in the event of an accident searchers would be unable to locate the victim.

Let us know
when you go
on our hills

Names and Addresses: Home Address and Local Address	Route
Time and date of departure:	Bad Weather Alternative:
Place of Departure and Registered Number of Vehicle (if any)	
Estimated time of return:	Walking/Climbing (delete as necessary)

GO UP WELL EQUIPPED – TO COME BACK SAFELY

Please tick items carried:

Emergency Food	Torch	Ice Axe
Waterproof Clothing (Colour-	Whistle	Crampons
Winter Clothing (Colour-	Map	Polybag
	Compass	First Aid

Please complete and leave with Police, landlady, warden etc.
Inform landlady or warden to contact Police if you are overdue.
PLEASE REPORT YOUR SAFE RETURN.

Companion volumes to *The Welsh Peaks*
by W. A. Poucher

The Lakeland Peaks
214 photographs, 14 maps, 141 routes
'An excellent guide . . . Should be compulsory—as well as
fascinating—reading for all climbers, ramblers and fell
walkers, to be studied and enjoyed before, during and
after every outing' *Cumberland Evening Star*

The Scottish Peaks
205 photographs, 31 maps, 73 routes
'Can be described as nothing less than "a monumental
work". The book is beautifully produced and is of a convenient size. I cannot conceive of a rucksack in Scotland
without a copy of *The Scottish Peaks* in a corner' *The
Climber*

'First-class guidebook for climbers and serious walkers . . .
The pictures have an aesthetic as well as a functional
quality. Anyone setting out for Scotland with mountains
in view should take Mr. Poucher's book in his pocket'
Sunday Times

The Peak & Pennines
200 photographs, 23 maps, 52 routes
' . . . thorough and inclusive of the whole "backbone of
England" (not forgetting the Pennine Way) and covers
equipment, route finding, useful centres both in the Peak
and Pennine areas, distances and times. It will slip easily
into a rucksack and provide hours of good reading after a
day's walking is over . . . superb photographs' *Dalesman*